Praise for *Academic Branding* and Dr. Sheena Howard

"This book is the compass that every person in academia needs in order to share their expertise with the world, using step-by-step instructions in order to achieve their dreams. While the job market might be difficult and higher education might not pay as well as you want it to, your blueprint for financial success is embedded in these pages. Your dreams are waiting."

—Michael Ayalon, CEO of Greek University

"*Academic Branding* provides a clear methodology, informed by best practices in teaching and learning, that scaffolds the personal and professional branding process for academics—allowing faculty to begin the process with thinking and exercises that lay the psychological and practical foundation for success in areas where faculty routinely struggle: building connection and community with those outside of academia and knowing your worth. This is an absolute must-read for minoritized faculty and graduate students!"

—Brea M. Heidelberg, PhD, associate professor and principal of ISO Arts Consulting

"*Academic Branding* is a must-have guide for faculty looking to increase the visibility and broader impact of their work. In her book, Dr. Howard clearly lays out the mindset, strategies, and action items that can help you cut through the noise and become a go-to authority in your field."

—Lindsay Tan, MFA, award-winning author and researcher, academic entrepreneur, and executive design strategist

"The Power Your Research program created by Dr. Sheena Howard could be your opportunity to dramatically increase not only your impact but your income. Lead by Dr. Howard, you'll develop and implement your own strategic communications marketing strategy to increase your visibility, authority, and ultimately your income. When you choose Dr. Howard and the Power Your Research program to shape your professional vision, your future is guaranteed to be bright and prosperous. I cannot recommend Dr. Sheena Howard and her Power Your Research process enough."

—Mark Kanty, president of Release Dynamics

"Dr. Sheena Howard's Power Your Research encourages educators to break down their four-wall domiciles to transform their research from lecture and conference papers to public conversation. She empowers the teacher to leave the desk or podium to step center stage and become a charismatic change agent."

—Dr. JL Adolph, assistant professor of English at Georgia State University

Academic

BRANDING

Also by Dr. Sheena C. Howard

Black Comics: Politics of Race and Representation (2013)

Black Queer Identity Matrix: Towards an Integrated Queer of Color Framework (2014)

Critical Articulations of Race, Gender, and Sexual Orientation (2014)

Encyclopedia of Black Comics (2017)

Why Wakanda Matters (2021)

Academic

BRANDING

A Step-by-Step Guide to Increased Visibility, Authority, and Income

CREATED BY: DR. SHEENA C. HOWARD
POWERED BY: POWER YOUR RESEARCH

BenBella Books, Inc.
Dallas, TX

BenBella Books, Inc.
10440 N. Central Expressway
Suite 800
Dallas, TX 75231
benbellabooks.com
Send feedback to feedback@benbellabooks.com

BenBella is a federally registered trademark.

Printed in the United States of America
10 9 8 7 6 5 4 3 2 1

Library of Congress Control Number: 2023034718
ISBN (hardcover) 9781637744406
ISBN (electronic) 9781637744413

Copyediting by Scott Calamar
Proofreading by Cape Cod Compositors, Inc. and Marissa Wold Uhrina
Indexing by WordCo Indexing Services
Text design and composition by PerfecType, Nashville, TN
Cover design by Morgan Carr
Printed by Lake Book Manufacturing

*In gratitude to every reader who embarks on this journey—
may this book inspire you to break barriers.*

Contents

Introduction

The book you hold in your hands is a culmination of everything I've learned over a decade of building my personal academic brand. The phrase "personal academic brand" may sound strange at first. In today's world, we are used to hearing about businesses as brands or even personal brands. However, an academic brand might not be something you've ever considered.

Many of us in higher education have forgotten that we have value outside of academia. I know this because I have worked in academia as a faculty member for over twenty years. I started my PhD program at Howard University at the age of twenty-three, right after I earned my master's degree. I am a product of all the highs and lows of the United States educational system. One year after graduating with my doctorate in intercultural and rhetorical communication, I landed a tenure-track job. Eventually, I went on to earn tenure, and then I became a full professor.

However, my desire to impact people outside of academia makes me different from a lot of other academics. And yet, early on in my academic career, I learned that I could not talk to my academic peers about my desire to increase my visibility and media coverage and translate my research for a mass audience. It was looked down upon by most academics, and I would hear things like: *You can't do real research if you are always on television.* I'm thankful I never bought into that.

Today, I am at a significant advantage because the online world that we engage in is all about building a brand to increase employability and marketplace value and for the generation of income. Over the last decade and a half, I have been featured on every media outlet you can think of—ABC, NPR, NBC, BBC. I have been in the *Washington Post* and the *Los Angeles Times*. My books have been mentioned on *Good Morning America,* in *the New York Times,* and beyond. Through my trials and tribulations of landing media spots, pitching op-eds, and publishing feature pieces, I have learned a great deal. I have a marketing degree that has come in handy as well. I have always enjoyed marketing myself. The thrill of convincing a producer of a well-known show to feature me on a segment makes me light up. It's like finishing a puzzle or mastering the psychology of persuasion for me. I know most people don't feel that way about self-promotion, which is why I created the Power Your Research program. This program is designed to help academics increase their visibility, authority, and income through one-on-one coaching sessions, access to a community of like-minded academics, and training modules. This book, which features many of the components of this program, will change your life if you implement the strategies and do the work.

There are two reasons I have written this book. The first is that I believe the world is a better place when subject-matter experts have the microphone. I know that many of my academic and educator friends do not have the know-how to build a platform. They struggle to use social media to translate their work for the masses. They are at a loss as to how to make money outside of academia, even though they have so much to offer beyond the classroom. This book will teach anyone with a master's degree or PhD how to increase their visibility, authority, and income without spending thousands a month on a publicist.

The second reason I wrote this book is that I know all too well how scary it can be to rely solely on academe to feed your family. With academic institutions struggling to keep enrollments steady, and the masses seeking alternative paths to education, there is nothing stable about your higher-ed job or tenure-track position. Moreover, those with advanced degrees who never found a home in academia need a pathway to financial freedom as well. If that is you, this book will change your life.

This book is broken down into three sections.

Part I is "Clarity." The Clarity section includes Chapters 1 through 4.

Chapter 1: "The Power Your Research Process" provides clarity on how this book parallels my Power Your Research program and how this book will guide you through the process of building your brand.

Chapter 2: "Mindset Matters" covers the stories we tell ourselves, and how those stories are holding us back. It delves into reframing the way you think about self-promotion and our limiting self-beliefs around money.

Chapter 3: "Your Vision" teaches you how to think beyond a collection of goals centered around higher education. This chapter gets you to nail down your life purpose, mission, and vision so you can use the rest of the book to achieve your big goals.

Coming out of Chapter 4: "Brand Assets," you will have your brand statement, which is connected to your purpose statement and vision. You will know your brand adjectives and brand archetype so you can nail down the messaging needed to connect with your target audience. These brand assets are going to set you on a path toward creating an impressive platform and giving you the clarity you need to succeed in translating your work for a mass audience. This chapter will also position you for the next section, "Connection," which will teach you how to build community and engage with your community in the online space and beyond.

Part II—"Connection" includes Chapters 5 through 7.

Chapter 5: "Social Media Strategy" teaches you how to use social media to activate your fan base. This is where you will learn how to establish a social media strategy that helps you reach your target audience. You will learn how to move from the professor who views people as an audience to the leader who builds a community.

Chapter 6: "Media Coverage" will teach you two Power Your Research strategic frameworks for getting major media coverage. You will learn how to use that coverage to position you to increase your income, deliver value, and turn followers into fans.

Chapter 7: "Visibility" focuses on understanding how to build credibility by accessing platforms that establish you as an authority in your field. Specifically, you will learn the system to land a TEDx talk and get your books into brick-and-mortar stores.

These two sections, "Clarity" and "Connection," will provide the essential building blocks needed to increase your revenue and turn your brand into a six-figure business. Thus, "Capital" is the final section of this book.

In Chapter 8: "1,000 True Fans," you will learn how to activate the people you have been connecting with, which in turn will allow you to provide value to them and make money. You will learn that with the "1,000 True Fans" strategy, the sky is the limit when it comes to monetizing your brand.

Finally, in Chapter 9: "The Sales Funnel," you will learn how to create a pathway to increase your revenue consistently and effectively by coming up with systems that make sense for your particular revenue streams.

As you can see, this book is comprehensive, and I'm so excited about your journey. I cannot wait to see your results as you move through the process. As you implement the strategies in this book, please share your progress with me on Instagram, Threads, LinkedIn, or X (formerly known as Twitter) at DrSheenaHoward. Do not hesitate to connect with other like-minded academics inside the Power Your Research Facebook group: www.facebook.com/groups/poweryour research. In addition, feel free to reach out directly to me at sheena@ poweryourresearch.com with your questions and comments. I'm happy to help!

PART I

Clarity

CHAPTER 1

The Power Your Research Process

First, I want to thank you for picking up this book. I know you will go through a transformational change if you follow the process that I have laid out for you. You will be learning how to go from where you are today to making an impact at scale and monetizing that impact along the way. I'm excited to take you on this journey. In order to set you up to successfully increase your visibility, authority, and income by leveraging your academic credentials, this chapter will first clarify some important components of the Power Your Research process. In this chapter, we will cover:

- What an academic brand is
- The Power Your Research process for building a brand
- How that process is laid out in this book
- Why the Power Your Research process was created
- Where this book begins in the Power Your Research process

Through covering these items you will get to know more about me and how my values are grounded in this process through my experience as an academic, entrepreneur, and mother who had to learn the value of my knowledge in the marketplace. As an entrepreneur, the story behind a product or service is critical to potential consumers. So in this chapter, you will see me being up-front and honest about the state of higher ed and working on a college campus. You will also learn that I am unapologetic about charging what I am worth for speaking engagements, consulting, and services I provide. You will come to learn more about me in this chapter and as you move through the Power Your Research process.

It's important to first understand what a brand is, so that you are clear on what you are getting into and what it might look like for you, your goals, and your career as an academic.

WHAT IS AN ACADEMIC BRAND?

As researchers, we know that operational definitions are critical to making sure our readers are on the same page. This is why I have dedicated a number of pages here to making sure you understand the terminology that will be critical to the process you are embarking on.

You'll hear me say "academic brand" a lot on my socials, and I refer to Power Your Research as an "academic branding" company. This means that Power Your Research does one thing: It helps academics build their brand. It's not for everyone; it's for you. When I refer to this process being for "academics," I mean that it is for anyone who has a master's degree or PhD. For me, an academic is not necessarily someone who teaches on a college campus. You've dedicated significant time to becoming a subject-matter expert in your area of expertise by furthering your education and thus, Power Your Research considers you an academic.

Power Your Research has served over one hundred people in the last two years, and while the program is marketed to "tenured professors," half of those in the program are simply those with advanced degrees with no aspirations of receiving tenure or being a full-time faculty member. The other half of my clients are tenure-track or tenured faculty. Both groups have had tremendous success implementing the Power Your Research process. You will get to know some of them as you read through this book.

Now that you know what I mean when I say "academic," I want to get clear on my definition of what it means to have "a brand." Building an academic brand simply means leveraging your academic credentials to increase your visibility, authority, and income. In that way, an academic brand is the same as a personal brand—it's simply designed for those who identify as academics. We have unique frames of reference, worldviews, and training as people who have spent a significant amount of time in the educational system. As you will learn throughout this book, while education is an amazing asset, some of this educational training can hinder us when it comes to brand building.

I will use "academic brand" and "personal brand" interchangeably because your academic brand is your personal brand. It's you! You just have credentials many others do not. Therefore, a personal brand is a representation of an individual's skills, values, and experiences. It is the sum of all the interactions between an individual and their audience. A personal brand can be created through social media channels, such as LinkedIn or X, and it can be created through blogging or other forms of content creation. The goal of a personal brand is to create a unique identity that will attract a specific audience to you. An individual's personal brand consists of their values, personality, and professional experience. These elements are all brought together to create a unique identity that sets the individual apart from their peers and competitors. When we add "academic" to it, we simply mean doing the aforementioned by building off of your academic credentials, as having an advanced degree already establishes a certain level of credibility that differentiates you in the marketplace. Your degree is an asset.

It's important to identify what you want your personal brand to represent and then make sure that everything you do aligns with that. This is the point of establishing your brand identity. This section focuses on your brand statement, brand archetype, and brand adjectives as the elements that will make up your brand identity. Being in alignment means that everything you put out into the world complements each other. This will include the images you use, the words you use, and even the products or services you offer. For example, if your personal brand is all about being fun and cheerful, then it would be important for your website to have a bright color scheme and be filled with pictures of people having fun.

The end result of a strong brand is that your name is connected to the keywords you want to be known for. My dissertation was on Black comics, such as superheroes and comic strips. Because I have been building my brand for over ten years around this topic, nearly anyone in the world can type "Black comics" into Google, and something about me will come up on the first or second page. Most likely, but not always, my book *Black Comics: Politics of Race and Representation* will come up in the book strip at the top of the results. If you're fact-checking this, the book is red and black and will probably be alongside some other books about the topic. If I were to stop talking about topics related to Black comics, my recognition in terms of the Google search engine would decline. It's competitive out there, so you need to maintain a level of visibility over the long haul if you want to maintain brand awareness.

A brand attaches your name to the keywords you want to be known for. People associate brands with particular messages. If I say "Snickers," you will automatically think about the phrase, "Hungry? Why wait?" The good news is this book will take you on a step-by-step journey for you to do the same, without the fluff. Now that you know what a brand is, we will move on to covering exactly what the Power Your Research process is and how that process is laid out for you in this book.

WHAT IS THE POWER YOUR RESEARCH PROCESS?

Power Your Research is a nine-step system for academics to increase their visibility, authority, and income without the expense of a publicist. These nine steps are a result of my brand-building process over ten years in which I have been able to create a multi-six-figure brand and land on major media outlets without paying a publicist to do so. In addition to my own personal experience, before creating this program, I had informally helped many of my academic friends land major media spots and increase their income by doing very simple things that you will learn in this book.

ON HIRING A PUBLICIST

I want to stop here to note that I do not have any problems with hiring a publicist, and in fact, after doing the work to build my brand, I did briefly hire one to get me to the finish line of a few high-level media opportunities in 2016. However, this was after I did the work of building my brand and landing several major media spots on my own so that I had something for the publicist to work off of. The problem is that far too many people think negatively about publicists because they pay them thousands of dollars but have nothing to help the publicist build from. They simply expect the publicist to do way more than they are actually intended to do and walk away with a nasty perception. In my experience, you only need to hire a publicist when you have contacts that you can pitch that are high level, and you want representation to close the deal. Even still, having a publicist is not a requirement; simply building relationships with producers is. You can do that on your own.

Before hiring a publicist, you want to clarify some things, such as who your audience is, what they want from you, and what you can offer. You also need to show that you can earn media coverage for the amazing things you have already done and continue to do. This means that 99 percent of the people reading this book do not need to spend thousands of dollars a month on a publicist who will likely only be able to get you a few media spots because you have nothing for them to turn into a successful pitch. If you can't successfully pitch yourself to FOX, NPR, BBC, and the like, then someone else cannot do it for you. You need to first do the work in this book before pursuing that option.

To give you a bit more context, my stint with a publicist, out of the almost fifteen years I have been doing this, has been one year. Therefore, follow the process in this book before you go out and spend thousands, only to be disappointed and discouraged.

The Power Your Research program consists of the following nine steps:
1. Mindset
2. Vision
3. Brand building
4. Media strategy
5. Media placements
6. Media blitz
7. Monetize
8. Build equity
9. Protect your future

This book is modeled from these steps in the same order. Since working with clients one-on-one is a bit different from writing it all out in a book, some of those steps have been modified or have received a name change. You can think of the nine chapters of this book as the nine steps of the actual program but reconfigured and reshaped to make sense for the reader. I cannot give you each and every scenario that I would be able to communicate to my clients face-to-face or in video modules inside the program, but the road map laid out here is all of what the Power Your Research program offers, and it will get you to six figures as well as help you build a platform you can be proud of.

Next, we will go over the high points of the steps of the Power Your Research program and how those steps translate to the content and road map in this book. After that, you will have clarity about the journey you are about to embark on. I will go over how each step of the Power Your Research program translates to what you are reading in this book by starting with this first step.

Mindset

We start here in both the program and this book because we do not want to pour water into a cup with holes. Having a master's degree or PhD means that we've learned many things in academia that are diametrically opposed to being an entrepreneur. Make no mistake: building a brand is about learning entrepreneurship.

In academia, having someone else write your research paper is called cheating. However, in business, having a social media manager write your captions is called outsourcing. Thus, there are many mindset shifts you need to address before implementing any of the branding strategies that will be covered here.

The best place to begin when it comes to mindset is finding a community. You'll want to get yourself into a community of other academics who believe in the importance of building a brand or at least find a community of support around your aspirations. You can find your own community of support, or you are welcome to join the Power Your

Research group online, which at the time of writing this book, is on Facebook and LinkedIn.

Vision

Wanting to build a brand is a great aspiration, but we cannot keep it all in our heads. We have to have a vision for our life that we can articulate. It must be written down—not for anyone else but for ourselves. If you are tenured, like me, you spent at least six years of your life doing things just to get tenure. I am sure you did those things because you wanted to, but it also prevented you from thinking about the things that bring you joy outside of higher education. In this step, we give you the space to identify what you want your life to look like one, two, and five years from now, outside of higher education.

In addition, this step involves detailing what amplifying your platform means for you. Too often, we get caught up in thinking we have to do what we see others do online, and that is not the case. When you start with your own vision, you can then build a strategy for making that vision come true. Building a brand is not about what someone else's life looks like; it is about what you want your life to look like. Your vision work is in Chapter 3, and it will teach you how to create your "why" statement so you can get the clarity you need before moving on to the next step.

Brand Assets

In this step of the Power Your Research process, you will identify your brand statement, brand archetype, and brand adjectives. To the average academic, these things probably do not sound that important, but we have to get clear on these things because you need to know who you want to show up as, who you want to reach, and why you want to reach them.

When hearing the phrase "brand assets," you most likely thought of things like logos and color schemes. While the Power Your Research program does consider these elements, this book does not focus on these because they are actually less important than the clarity you need in terms of your brand statement, brand archetypes, and brand adjectives. Once you have the latter you will actually more easily be able to identify what color schemes and logos will make sense for your brand's mission, vision, and purpose. Chapter 4 covers all three brand assets of the Power Your Research program.

Media Strategy and Media Placements

The media strategy and media placement steps of the Power Your Research process are Chapters 5, 6, and 7. This is where you will learn how to connect with the people who care about the things you care about. In this book, it will look like devising your social media strategy based on the strategy that I've identified for busy academics called the "3H system." It will demystify what you should be posting on socials, how often, and why. In addition, these chapters will cover strategic frameworks for getting low-, mid-, and high-level media placements by focusing on podcasts.

In the Power Your Research program we extensively cover all types of media placement strategies (such as TV, radio, etc.); however, because this book cannot cover each and every situation, we focus on podcasts due to the accessibility and popularity of the medium and because the tactics translate to all other media placement opportunities. You will learn that being successful in the podcast space will open doors to a variety of opportunities that will benefit your brand.

A NOTE

Step 6 of the Power Your Research process is called "media blitz"; however, that is not covered in this book as I have made the decision to focus on the aspects of the process that can be delivered in book format in the most efficient and effective way possible in order to help you get the results you are looking for as soon as possible. Media blitz simply did not translate well in book format, but if you follow Power Your Research on LinkedIn, Facebook, or X, I discuss this strategy in detail on my live videos and other free offerings.

Monetize, Build Equity, and Protect Your Future

These last three steps of the Power Your Research program are covered in Chapters 8 and 9. This phase of the Power Your Research program teaches you exactly what it suggests. That is, how to build a six-figure income off of your brand. Of course, everyone is monetizing something unique to them, and each and every situation cannot be addressed in a book; however, the selected strategies around monetization included in this book will get you to six figures when implemented properly, with an understanding that increasing your income requires learning these entrepreneurship skills and tailoring the information to your specific assets, audience, and expertise.

WHY I CREATED THE POWER YOUR RESEARCH PROCESS

The end goal of the Power Your Research process is to financially protect your future from an unstable higher education system. If you have an advanced degree, you can make six figures based on your academic credentials, passions, and talents. The reason it's important for me to teach academics how to do this is that I have been in the situation where I've seen faculty with tenure lose their jobs. I know there are people who graduated with PhDs, but after ten years they never landed that tenure-track job they dreamed of. I've worked with PhDs who are stuck in the adjunct and lecturer trap for decades.

In a 2023 article titled "The End of Faculty Tenure and the Transformation of Higher Education," Mark Stein states that "the long-term decline in tenure density threatens the future of higher education in blue and red states alike."[1] According to Stein, "In the last several decades, tenure density—the proportion of faculty members in tenured and tenure-track positions—has been declining in the United States. This decline now constitutes one of the greatest threats to higher education that the United States has ever experienced." In addition, research shows that there is about a 10 to 25 percent chance of a PhD getting a tenure-track job.

We have all heard the stories or suffered through them ourselves. You finish your dissertation, go on the job market a year before graduation, send out several job applications, and graduate thinking that eventually something will work out. But it doesn't. Thirty applications, maybe three in-person interviews, but zero offers. For the many that do not land a tenure-track position, they get stuck in the adjunct or lecturer circuit, where they are sometimes paid less than minimum wage.

Multiple studies have shown that depending on the discipline, as few as one fourth and as many as one half of PhDs get hired in academic jobs at all and that only a third of these jobs are on the tenure track.[2]

These trends are not turning around anytime soon, if ever. According to Arjun Chowdhury, since 2008, the number of assistant professor positions, the first permanent academic appointment for PhDs, has diminished by around 15 percent in Canada.[3] The numbers are no better in other countries around the world. Even as secure academic positions dwindle, the majority of PhDs continue to prefer academic employment and pursue poorly paid temporary academic positions in their efforts to obtain tenure-track positions.

Many of those who I graduated with spent years in the job market, bouncing around from institution to institution in an incredibly vicious cycle. Some left higher education altogether. Some eventually left higher education, even after getting tenure or a tenure-track job, due to toxic environments or dissatisfaction with their institutions.

The tenure-track job market is even tighter today than it was in 2010. In addition, for those with tenure, the idea of job security is misleading, in my opinion. We have a false sense of security around tenure that we are secretly afraid to acknowledge. I'd rather acknowledge it and protect myself than trick myself into a false reality that can bite me in the butt later.

Tenure is supposed to mean "a job for life," but over the last few years, programs have closed, departments have closed, and entire universities have closed, leaving even those with tenure back on the job market. At least thirty-four public or nonprofit colleges have closed, merged, or announced closures or mergers since March 2020. Campus closures peaked in the years leading up to the pandemic, driven by private for-profit college closures.[4]

In addition, the small percentage of people who have reached tenure and even full professor still have a problem on their hands. They realize that they are either not making the money they thought they would or that reaching the highest promotion means they have reached their pay ceiling. You cannot get a promotion after becoming a full professor; therefore, you need to become an administrator if you want to increase your income. Many academics do this for the money, not because they truly want to be an administrator on a college campus. I think this is a tragedy because anyone with academic credentials can build a six-figure brand and leave the impact they actually want to leave without becoming an administrator.

There is another way. You can make more money than your institution can pay you by building your brand. If you can make both academia and entrepreneurship work together, that's even better. Last

14

I checked, Brené Brown was still on faculty at her university. Lots of famous scholars remain connected to a university, whether it be teaching full-time or part-time.

MORE NUMBERS

Less than 17 percent of new PhDs in science, engineering, and health-related fields find tenure-track positions within three years after graduation.[5] In addition, for those who have found a tenure-track job and received tenure, unfortunately, that does not guarantee you a job for life, as some of my tenured friends might claim. According to Michael Kabbaz, even before the 2020 pandemic, Moody's had downgraded the financial viability of a growing number of American colleges.[6]

Kabbaz goes on to report that most private colleges can absorb an enrollment decline of 5 percent. Yet, data from the National Student Clearinghouse shows that the number of high school seniors matriculating directly into college fell by 21.7 percent in 2020. That means that a growing number of colleges will have to cut even more costs in order to preserve their credit ratings, which may very well accelerate the frequency of surprise closures in years to come.

Research has already shown that the number of available tenure-track positions is dwindling as well. Furthermore, having tenure will not save your job if your department, program, or university is cut or closes down.

AN EXAMPLE: THE JOB MARKET

Natalie Ruth Joynton tells the story of her search for a tenure-track position in a 2022 *Inside Higher Ed* article.[7] Natalie was two years into her job search, applying for tons of tenure-track jobs with no luck. She had been an adjunct with a PhD for years at her current university while she applied for full-time positions. She decided to try an online job ad and read a comment from someone that said, "It's okay to quit." Natalie was taken aback. However, soon after, she decided to apply for industry positions in her field as a writer.

She applied for some twenty jobs and was astonished to find how quickly she got a job offer. She describes the process of applying for jobs outside of academe as "straightforward and transparent." Natalie never did get that tenure-track job, according to the *Inside Higher Ed* article; she landed a job as a writer for a marketing department.

Unfortunately, Natalie's story is not rare.

We spend from about the age of eighteen to about the age of sixty-five working—nearly all of our life—and I choose to use those years to do work that I truly love, which is building my brand and teaching people. I want you to be able to do that as well. Many academics simply do not know how to do this because, as academics, we are not trained to think like entrepreneurs, even though, in many ways, we are well positioned to make money in the marketplace as our education differentiates us.

Building a brand requires you to think like the creative you are and the businessperson you will learn to be. This book will give you the road map to build that brand without the fluff. If you are a tenured faculty member reading this book, you do not have to abandon your day job. The Power Your Research process is designed to make that day job an option, not a thing of the past if you do not want it to be. That is, you can leave your faculty position if you want to, because you are able to make more money from your brand than any university can ever pay you. Having the option to leave is the magic of the Power Your Research process and why the last step of the road map is called "protect your future."

If you just want a few media placements and that's it, then the Power Your Research process is not for you. However, if you want to find your community, serve the people who you can help, and make an impact at scale, then you are in the right place. This is about increasing your visibility, authority, AND income. You will be learning a transformational life-changing skill set here.

Finally, I created this program because I think the world is a better place when subject-matter experts have the microphone. You are that subject-matter expert; you just need the tools and road map to help you succeed.

In today's fast-paced and technological world, people who are not subject-matter experts are positioning themselves as such because they are good at using social media and online tools to build a brand. They have the ability to disseminate information to a large number of people because they are master storytellers, brand builders, and entrepreneurs. They are out there talking about the same thing you got a master's degree or PhD in, but they are doing it bigger and better than you are. And they are making a ton of money. Unfortunately, they are not always disseminating factual information because they are not experts in the subjects they're representing.

This program empowers the average academic, the subject-matter expert, to be in a powerful position to reach a critical mass of people.

MY STORY

Currently, I am a full professor at a small liberal arts university. I was able to land a tenure-track position in 2011, when the United States economy was at its weakest. After graduating in 2010, I took a lecturer position in my first year out of graduate school for one year at Shippensburg University in Pennsylvania. During my time as a graduate student on the job market, I received one tenure-track position offer in

New York City, but I decided to turn it down and take a gamble with the lecturer position, hoping to get a better offer later. Thankfully, the gamble paid off, and I landed at an institution that supported me on my tenure journey. I am still at that institution more than ten years later. But I am not relying on my tenure for financial security, and I am here to show you another way.

During my time at this small university, we have had our fair share of financial difficulties. I have seen mergers, layoffs, and faculty leave the institution to go elsewhere out of fear of being laid off. I have been in the job market seeking employment when things looked especially doom and gloom.

Between declining enrollments, being a tuition-driven institution, and then the 2020 pandemic, things have looked especially bleak. It was during those tumultuous times that I also had my son, went through a divorce, and lost everything financially, thus propelling me to begin taking monetizing my brand seriously. I became afraid that if I lost my tenured position, I'd have no way to support my family. I became aware that tenure didn't mean a job for life, and while it provided some security, it wasn't a bulletproof plan to stay employed.

While I had been landing major media spots since my first article was published in graduate school, I hadn't been thinking like an entrepreneur. I always knew that I didn't want my research to sit behind an academic paywall, and with an undergraduate degree in marketing, I enjoyed convincing the media to have me on their programs. However, when it came to charging what I was worth for speaking engagements and other paid opportunities, I just wasn't thinking about being financially independent. I'd speak all over the country for free or for an honorarium, which means "no charge." However, my mindset around monetization had to change if I wanted to live in abundance instead of fear in the unstable world of higher education.

I had worked hard for tenure and to become a full professor, and I didn't want to spend the rest of my life fearful that I could lose it all if my university or program closed (I was actually terrified of this very thing). Additionally, with "full professor" being the pay ceiling, I didn't want to struggle financially to give my son the life he deserved. One solution was to take the brand I had built and monetize it. But before I could do that, I had to learn entrepreneurship the same way I learned how to become a successful academic. Mindset shift was the first step.

I had to stop feeling bad about increasing my rates. I could not feel bad about seeking even larger media placements. I could not feel bad about selling my books out loud and up close. I could not worry about what my colleagues would think. I could not be scared of trolls on social media. I had to let those things go if I really wanted to get out from under the fear of losing my job and the pay ceiling I was stuck under.

As academics, we do not like the sound of "sales" or "self-promotion." However, I learned that self-promotion isn't about me. It's about the lives out there that I want to impact. And if I want to make an impact, I have to make money along the way.

Once I built a six-figure brand and informally helped my academic friends build their brands, I developed Power Your Research, the nine-step system to increased visibility, authority, and income without the expense of a publicist.

Now, let's begin *your* journey.

CHAPTER 2

Mindset Matters

The proper mindset is the very foundation of success on your journey to building a brand. Yet everyone has their own unique limiting self-beliefs and mental blocks to overcome.

The Power Your Research process starts with mindset. Just as a sturdy foundation is crucial for constructing a strong and stable building, addressing mindset issues is an essential building block in this process. Without the proper mindset around self-promotion, the value of increasing your income, and finding community, it will be hard to do the work required to increase your visibility, authority, and income.

This chapter covers how to reframe the way you think about self-promotion, how imposter syndrome impacts your mindset, and how you can find the communities outside of academia that support your goals. By the end of this chapter, you will also have created a strong purpose statement you can use as a vehicle to strengthen your new mindset shifts.

The mindset shifts covered in this chapter have been selected because, after working with academics over the last decade, I've found these to be the most prevalent mental roadblocks I have worked through with clients. In addition, I have had to overcome all of these as well. They are presented in this chapter in no particular order, as they are all essential to address before moving on to the more tangible work of building your brand as an academic.

THE SELF-PROMOTION MINDSET

Many academics come to me looking to figure out how they can get their work in front of more people. However, many are also uncomfortable promoting themselves. That is, they don't like talking about themselves, their accomplishments, and even their hopes and dreams. If you are a faculty member, it might even feel taboo to talk about the fact that you want your work in front of a wider audience. I've heard the grumblings of people who say, "If you're on TV talking about your work, that means you aren't a real researcher."

Before I was a tenured professor, I was part of an online group where you could seek advice. I posted that I wanted to get on national TV shows and really be a superstar researcher for the work I was doing in comics. The comments were insulting, and some even called me a troll just because I was seeking advice on the issue. I felt humiliated. Thankfully, this didn't deter me from pursuing my dream of actually reaching the people I was researching as opposed to my work being stuck behind an academic paywall my entire life.

Let this book be a safe place for you to dream without judgment. There is nothing wrong with wanting to leave a bigger impact with your work. Doing media spots doesn't make you less of a researcher. You are not a troll for wanting to build a major brand. The online space allows you to reach millions of people who care about the work you are doing. Personally, the thought of my academic books and papers sitting in the basement of college libraries makes me sad. This is why I spent over a decade figuring out how to build an international brand

and then helping my fellow academics do the same. **It doesn't matter what your area of expertise is, you can do this.**

Academia makes us forget that we have value outside of higher education. It's a strange thought. After a few years, even faculty who come from industry into a tenure-track position forget that they have value outside of academia. Is it in the water we drink?

But before you can become a thought leader, you need to reframe the way you think about self-promotion. **Self-promotion is NOT about YOU.** Even though the phrase has the word "self" in it, it's actually about the people you can help and give value to. You need to promote yourself so that the people who need to hear from you can find you. Otherwise, they will never know you exist. There is someone somewhere right now looking for you and your expertise. You have a knowledge base they care about, but they cannot find you.

And this is the mindset shift you need to make immediately. Your visible presence will allow people to dream and better their lives, but again, they cannot find you. These are all reasons you need to stop feeling icky about self-promotion.

One key step at this juncture is to not even think about making money. Just think about self-promotion as a way of helping people find you, so you can help them. This should take the pressure off feeling like you are selling anything. So, until we get further along in this process, just think about how you can assist people instead of feeling like your mission is to sell yourself or your product or service. Later we will learn about monetization, but it's easier to overcome this self-promotion mindset issue now by understanding the importance of giving value rather than promoting anything other than how you can help others.

Until now, you've probably only thought of your work in terms of how it can get you tenure or a job. Now, you've reset your resistance to self-promotion by focusing on how you can help and serve people first. The way to make money is to be of service to people, not by prioritizing how you can make money off people. Isn't that ironic?

23

My Story

I never thought about becoming a college professor as a kid. I received my master's degree from New York Institute of Technology in 2007. While there, I studied graphic design and began teaching computer applications as my first full-time job. It was then that I realized I wanted to teach full-time, even though I disliked that particular job. It wasn't the act of teaching that was stressful; it was the organization itself.

Upon graduating with my master's, I promised myself that if I was going to teach for a living, I was going to try to make sure I was not only happy but also well compensated for my work. That's when I decided to apply to Howard University for my PhD studies. Up until this point, I'd had only two Black college professors. I had only one Black woman professor my entire college career, which was four years for my undergraduate degree and two years for my master's. The Black male professor I had was an adjunct, not full-time. For me, being a full-time professor felt like a pipe dream, not something that I thought could actually happen for me. That is, until I got to Howard University and saw a campus full of Black professors—of all genders. That's when I knew I could do it. That's when I knew that I could be one too.

I share this backstory to illustrate a point that is bigger than just getting my work in front of more people. For me, building an international brand means that there is someone, somewhere in the world, who doesn't even realize they can be a professor or a comic book writer or a creative entrepreneur like me. And if I don't continue this work, I may never reach that individual. I want to give them hope, inspiration, and a road map to show them what's possible. I think about this in terms of my place in the world but also in terms of the actual things I study and create.

Back in 2007, when I told my professors I wanted to do my dissertation on Black comic strips, they weren't impressed. Not many were studying comics back then, and it wasn't taken seriously in academia.

24

I actually had an upperclassman tell me that my existence in the program devalued her PhD. Looking back on those moments reminds me why I am passionate about getting my work in front of the masses. Doing so means that I can be an inspiration to other academics who are made to feel like their work does not have value. In addition, my work has been able to empower young people to believe in themselves and pursue their dreams even when it's scary or lonely.

If I was simply thinking of self-promotion as something to put money in my pockets, I wouldn't have been successful. People can feel your intentions when they read your work or see you in interviews. What does that mean for you? **It means that you need to understand that talking about yourself, your work, and your accomplishments is bigger than you.**

An Example: Why Self-Promotion Matters

In fact, as I am writing this book, I just jumped off a coaching call with a woman who does research on foster kids. That is such a powerful area of interest that can really change an entire population's life, outlook, and future. However, her branding work needs to be done so that she can get her knowledge out to the masses—the organizations that work with this population, the individual kids in foster care, and the media outlets that care about this area of expertise.

Her work has so much value, but right now, it's unfortunately stuck behind an academic paywall. Her research is published in high-level journal articles that people have to pay for or be on a college campus to access. Worse yet, academic articles are not written for regular people. No one outside of higher education wants to read your journal article with a dictionary in hand. From today on, I need you to think about self-promotion as the lives you want to impact and the people you want to help.

Reframing Your Self-Promotion Mindset

Here are my steps for how you can reframe your mindset about self-promotion:

1. Understand that self-promotion isn't at all about you.
2. Understand why your work is important and to whom it is important.
3. Understand that your very existence and what you study are unbelievably important to others.
4. Once you feel steps 1 through 3 in your soul (and believe them), get out there and start talking about the amazing things you do.

Paraphrasing Mahdi Woodard, an amazing marketer I follow online: "If you can make it out of your own head, you can make it anywhere." Much of building an incredible brand requires you to get out of your comfort zone, address limiting self-beliefs, and confront your insecurities.

USE YOUR INSTITUTION'S MEDIA TEAM

I was fortunate enough to get my first tenure track position at a small liberal arts university that valued both teaching and research. In addition, they supported me in building a brand based on my work. They invited the media coverage and visibility I would get. In fact, my clients who are in academe are pleasantly surprised that when they start doing the work I teach them to get more media coverage, their institution's media team is delighted to help them. I invite you, whether you are in academia or not, to stop creating false narratives in your head about the support you may or may not get.

IMPOSTOR SYNDROME

The next mindset shift is something that virtually every academic I come across needs to address: the dreaded impostor syndrome.

Impostor syndrome is a mindset issue that seeps into many aspects of the brand-building process, if you let it. It can completely destroy your chances of building an incredible brand if you do not properly redirect it to fuel your success instead of hindering it.

Impostor syndrome is more common among high-achieving individuals who have been praised for their intelligence and abilities. It can also be triggered by the fear of being exposed as a "fraud" or "impostor." The term was coined by clinical psychologists Dr. Pauline Rose Clance and Suzanne Imes in 1978. A person with impostor syndrome may worry that they will be exposed as fraudulent or that their achievements are the result of luck or circumstance rather than true talent. They may feel the need to constantly prove themselves, to be seen as worthy of the praise they have received.

In some cases, "impostors" believe that others are better than they are and can easily see through their efforts. This feeling can become so overwhelming that it leads them to hide their work from others and make excuses for why it isn't good enough.

Why do people feel this way? People with impostor syndrome often believe their success is a fluke and that everyone else around them is more accomplished and smarter than they are. They think that the people who seem to be succeeding are actually better than them, so rather than take credit for their successes, they assume that everything is a sham.

When Impostor Syndrome Kicks In

Impostor syndrome likely kicks in for you when you do something you've never done before or start to dream about building an incredible brand. You may think, "I can't do that" or "my research isn't important," or "no one will ever pay me $10,000 for a speaking engagement."

Here's the thing about impostor syndrome: It is normal. When you are doing or attempting to do something you've never done before, you will come up against that feeling of being an impostor because you've never done that thing before!

Your first big TV interview on ABC news may bring up feelings of impostor syndrome because it's new. You're in disbelief that you'll actually be featured on ABC news. I like to sum up the way to confront impostor syndrome by using the words of entrepreneur Alex Hormozi. He says, "You don't become confident by shouting affirmations in the mirror, but by having a stack of undeniable proof that you are who you say you are. Outwork your self-doubt." This is powerful. Alex Hormozi has scaled and exited seven companies. His most notable exit was the majority sale of his licensing company for $46.2 million in 2021. He talks a lot about overcoming limiting self-beliefs on his platform. This one quote from Hormozi addresses one of the best ways to confront those feelings of being an impostor.

During your work here, impostor syndrome is going to come up. You will feel it. I felt it writing this book. I felt it when I did my first TEDx talk. I've felt it on some of my biggest interviews. I've felt it all the way up the ladder to success (and I continue to feel it), but in all those instances, **I never let it stop me.**

My mission is always more important than the fear I experience. And along the way, I look back on all the things I've accomplished as a reminder that I deserve all of the opportunities that I am blessed with. If you're in the room, you deserve to be there. So the best way to address impostor syndrome is by doing the work and getting the receipts. That is, the receipts are the proof you need to confront that voice in your head. Confront the voice that's telling you that you can't do something or that you don't deserve something by doing the work and building the proof. Impostor syndrome can also look like the excuses you are telling yourself or the fictional roadblocks you are creating.

An Example: Combating Impostor Syndrome

I had a coaching call with a client recently. She wants to create her own coaching program to help K through 12 educators better work with diverse learners. I always address mindset on the first call with my clients. The very first thing my client, let's call her Suzie, said she wanted to work on was her confidence. She had two main areas of concern.

First, she felt that the book she was about to publish wasn't good enough because it wasn't with a top-tier academic publisher. Second, she felt that if she started a coaching program, she might not be able to work with all of the people who would be signing up to join her program.

I pointed out to her that her first concern was really about impostor syndrome. She felt she didn't have enough credibility, even though she has a PhD in the area and has an upcoming book with a traditional publisher. Yet, the feedback loop in her head is still telling her she isn't good enough. I was there to remind her that she is fully qualified, and we spent time breaking down the statistics on how many people actually have a PhD in teacher education, as that makes her more credible than even people with only a master's degree in that field (let alone the people teaching in that area without even any graduate school credentials).

One way to overcome negative thoughts is to work with a coach who can intercept the negative feedback loop. Or get into a community of people who give you positive reinforcement. Her second concern was about being nervous that she wouldn't be able to serve all of the people joining her program. I reminded her that she is trying to solve a problem in her head that she doesn't have yet. She doesn't even know if she will have too many people in her program to coach. That's a problem she can tackle when it happens. However, this goes back to confidence. **When we create a problem in our head that we do not yet have, we are giving ourselves permission to stop pursuing the thing we say we want.**

In simple terms, Suzie felt she wasn't good enough to create a coaching program and serve people. Outside of intercepting those types of thoughts and being around people who can break that negative feedback loop, you can also give yourself space to acknowledge what you have already accomplished—that is, acknowledging the proof we already have or creating more proof.

Hang It on the Wall

One thing that really helps with creating this undeniable proof that says you are who you say you are is to create places where you hang your accomplishments on the wall. I made it a point to get nearly all of my significant certificates, degrees, awards, and accomplishments framed. I took those frames and put them on a wall in a corner of my room where my desk is. I cannot sit at my desk without being surrounded by my past accomplishments. I did this same thing in my office at work. I don't just have my degrees on the wall, but also my trophies from when I was a kid, including any gold medals I won. Nearly all of my accomplishments are in these key environments of my life that remind me consciously and subconsciously that I am good enough. I encourage you to do the same for yourself on this journey.

Impostor Syndrome and Money

One of the many areas I see impostor syndrome holding clients back is when it comes to making money. What you think about making money and increasing your income is going to be critical to attaining the end goal of the Power Your Research process. The process won't work if you do not see the value of increasing your income. In addition, the foundation of Power Your Research is to protect the future of academics as academia becomes more and more unstable in terms of job security. When clients reach me, some of them are all about learning how to increase their income through building a brand, and others say things like "I don't care about money" or "I don't want to make money." If money is not important to you, then the Power Your Research process is not for you.

I spent years creating things using my own money, not thinking about my art as a business. I had the mindset that if I wanted something in the world, it was okay to go broke bringing it to life. We've all done this. If you've ever done a speaking engagement in which you didn't get paid or you only got paid $500 to $1,000, you know what I mean. This needs to be nipped in the bud right now if you really want to become a thought leader. You cannot leave an impact and reach more people if you do not make money while doing it.

That means you need to increase your prices. You need to charge more for consulting jobs. You need to start thinking about brand building as a business, not something you're willing to go broke doing. I spent years going broke building my brand in the beginning. You do not need to make that same mistake. I know you probably have already done your fair share of free and low-paid speaking engagements. You probably keep coming up with reasons why you need to do more speaking engagements for free or at a low cost. Or worse, you might be telling yourself that "no one will pay me more" for a speaking engagement or consulting gig. That is a limiting self-belief, and it is false.

Let's look at the simple word "honorarium." Lots of my academic and educator friends get asked to do talks for an honorarium. From the Oxford Reference website, the definition of an honorarium is "a payment given for professional services that are rendered nominally without charge." That means every engagement that you did for an honorarium, you weren't intended to actually be paid. An honorarium isn't payment. When someone asks you to do a speaking engagement for an honorarium, they are asking you to do it for free.

Right now, there are thousands of speakers who do not have an advanced degree who are getting paid $5,000, $7,000, and $10,000-plus for a one-hour talk that you are doing for free. Do you know why you're doing that? Because of the following:

1. Academe has convinced you this is normal. (Academe trains us to have impostor syndrome.)
2. You suffer from impostor syndrome. (You keep creating reasons why you need to do engagements for free.)
3. You have a scarcity mindset. (You're scared to ask for more, aka impostor syndrome.)

When you can keep impostor syndrome under control or use it to your advantage, you have less fear around being seen online, increasing your speaking engagement rates, increasing your consultant rates, and starting that program you always wanted to start. This mindset shift is also an essential component in the monetization phase of the Power Your Research process.

FINDING COMMUNITY

Being part of a community that supports your goals is a powerful tool in changing your mindset and achieving success. It is something that you need to seek out immediately, which is why I am dedicating this section to it. Here are some ways in which a supportive community will help on your mindset journey:

1. **Motivation and Accountability:** A supportive community can provide motivation and accountability for achieving goals. When you're surrounded by people who are working toward similar goals, it can be easier to stay focused and motivated. You may also feel more accountable to the group, which can help you stay on track.

2. **Resources and Information:** A supportive community can provide access to resources and information that can help you achieve your goals. For example, if you're trying to start a business, being part of an entrepreneurial community can give you access to mentors, investors, and other resources that can help you succeed.

3. **Collaboration and Networking:** Being part of a supportive community can provide opportunities for collaboration and networking. This can lead to partnerships and connections that can help you achieve your goals. You may also learn new skills and ideas from others in the community.

4. **Emotional Support:** Pursuing goals can be challenging, and having a supportive community can provide emotional support when things get tough. You can turn to others for advice, encouragement, and empathy, which can help you stay motivated and resilient.

Being part of the right communities will give you access to not only social support but resources and social capital as well. According to a study published in the *Journal of Innovation and Entrepreneurship*, it is well known that capital and resources are critical to entrepreneurial decisions. Family, relatives, friends, and social networks are an integral part of the game as social relationships offer further legitimacy to new ventures.[8]

Doing the work of building your brand is not something that is generally popular to talk about among your academic colleagues. Some will put their nose in the air at the mere mention of wanting to get media coverage and visibility. In fact, I have had clients report to me that after starting the Power Your Research process, colleagues have tried to sabotage them because they were jealous of the media attention and credibility they were getting as a result of doing the work.

This is why it is important to be around people who have a similar mission, vision, and purpose. Power Your Research has a membership community on Facebook for clients for this very reason. However, you do not need to think as narrowly as the Power Your Research community in terms of finding a space for yourself. I am a member of multiple communities that support me on my journey.

My clients are members of places like co-working spaces in their cities. Personally, I am a member of a speakers' bureau with fifteen to twenty other academics and nonacademics who all are looking to build their brands. We support each other. We share each other's content. We share networks. The CEO of my speakers' bureau is in alignment with my goals around building my brand.

As such, being part of a community that supports your goals can provide motivation, accountability, resources, collaboration, networking, and emotional support, all of which can help you achieve success.

One thing I want you to do right now is to start researching communities that might support you and then begin going to their meet-ups or become a member of those spaces. These should be outside of any college campus, as you are learning the journey of thinking outside of academia, so you need to connect with nonacademics.

PURPOSE STATEMENT

Now that we have covered the essential mindset shifts necessary to succeed using the Power Your Research method and have explored finding supportive communities, you need to have a solid mechanism to hold and stay firm in your newfound perspective.

The way to do that is to create a purpose statement. Your purpose statement is your "why" statement (I use these terms interchangeably). This is what you will use to support the mindset shifts discussed in this chapter and to help you stay the course when the process gets overwhelming and daunting.

Making mindset shifts, and then doing the hard work necessary to overcome those mental challenges and reach your goals, will require you to remember why this is important to you in the first place. Your purpose statement will allow you to operate in pursuit of your goals while out of your comfort zone, when you need to do so. While self-promotion, increasing your income, tapping into your creativity, staying motivated, and finding community might be new and scary, your purpose statement will help you stay the course to do those new and intimidating things.

Why the heck do you want to become a thought leader in the first place? The work is hard. It forces you to confront things you can easily ignore by continuing along as you are. The work will require a number of failures. It will mean dedicated time and energy. It will require you to set boundaries you currently do not have. You'll have to do all those uncomfortable tasks. And that means you need to have a strong purpose statement so that you do not give up when it gets tough.

My Why

On my LinkedIn platform, I go live a few times a week. Each year, I talk to over 150 people on one-on-one free sales calls. I coach over fifty academics a year on brand building. I do this in addition to being a professor and running a second writing business. I am also a single mom. So why do I do it? Why do I continue to show up for my academics even when I am tired? It's because I have a strong why statement. Without it, I would have given up long ago. I certainly wouldn't be sitting here, the day after the Thanksgiving holiday, writing this book. Yet here I am.

The outcome of my work is certainly financial. I make good money as a professor while running two businesses. My businesses are all a part of my brand vehicle that is financially protecting my future. However, my "why" is not specifically about money. If my why were only about the money, this journey would be unsustainable. If your why is only to increase your income, you'll fail. There's nothing wrong with money being the outcome you want or even for it to be a part of your desired outcome; however, money is the outcome of the outcome. It's the last thing that happens, after you power through showing up for yourself and your community. It is only after you show up consistently that you can even start to make some money or some impact. For context, an excerpt from my purpose statement is the following:

> *I am committed to achieving success on my terms because I want to show others that they can succeed even after they have made mistakes in their lives. I want to be a living example of a way forward. I also want to show and teach my son how to be resilient. It is a must for me to succeed because I am a single mother.*

Whenever I think about not showing up and doing the work, I reread my purpose statement; I don't check my bank account. I had to hang my purpose statement somewhere that I could see it every day until it was ingrained in my head. This is what you will need to do as well.

Your Purpose Statement (Your "Why") Exercise

Note: What follows is a modified version of a purpose statement exercise I learned in the Upscale Your Business program with my current business coaches Jaimie Skultety and Mark Kanty.

Now that you have an understanding of the importance of the why statement, it's time to create your own. Your purpose statement is personal to you, which is why I only shared an excerpt of mine in this book. To create your own, answer the following questions, and then arrange your answers in one or two paragraphs:

Why are you ABSOLUTELY committed to reaching success on your own terms?

Why is it a must for you, to the extent that you WILL do whatever it takes, for as long as it takes, and endure whatever is necessary, no matter how many ups and downs there may be, in order to get there?

Once you answer these two questions, arrange them together into one or two paragraphs until you have a solid purpose statement. For example, your answer to the first question might be:

Answer: I am absolutely committed to reaching success on my own terms because my parents worked so hard as schoolteachers, but they always lived paycheck to paycheck. While I had everything I needed as a child, my parents always worried about paying the bills, and as a result, it impacted the way I think about money. I don't want my kids to feel insecure about money or the impact they can make in the world.

Your answer to the second question might be:

Answer: My research is about advocating for the rights of people who, as adults, have found out they were adopted. As someone who found out I was adopted at the age of thirty-three, I had to fight to find my biological mother. The names of my biological parents were sealed, and it was very challenging for me to go on that journey. It impacted me physically and mentally. I will endure whatever is necessary for me to succeed because I want to prevent every adult I can from going through the trials and tribulations that I went through in order to find closure after finding out they were adopted.

Putting these two answers together into your purpose statement might look like this:

> *I am absolutely committed to reaching success on my own terms because my parents worked so hard as schoolteachers, but they always lived paycheck to paycheck. While I had everything I needed as a child, my parents always worried about paying the bills, and, as a result, it impacted the way I think about money. I don't want my kids to feel insecure about money or the impact they can make in the world.*
>
> *As someone who found out I was adopted at the age of thirty-three years old, I had to fight to find my biological mother. It was a painful experience finding out, but knowing the system wouldn't give me the necessary information to aid me in finding my biological parents made it even more agonizing. It impacted me physically and mentally. Therefore, I will endure whatever is necessary and do whatever is necessary so that I can prevent every adult that faced my situation from going through what I went through all those years ago. I need to change the system so that I can change the lives of the people I care about.*

Once you have written this out, feel free to think about it for a couple of days. You can always tweak it so that it resonates more and more with you. You should really feel in your heart that it is true to you and meaningful for you.

When you are happy with your purpose statement, place it where you will see it every day as you do the work to build your brand. Internalize this statement to the point where it is a part of you, and you remember it (or the essence of it) without reading it. When you want to give up on doing the work we will cover in this book, you need to recall this statement and push through the feeling of wanting to stop or not show up. Even when you have to confront the fear of impostor syndrome or limiting self-beliefs, rely on this statement to overpower those thoughts so that you can push through.

The honest truth is that most people won't follow through on the work of getting the mega results they want, and ultimately, they will be stuck exactly where they are. That's why it's important to establish your "why" statement before jumping into the brand-building work that lies ahead in this book.

Now that you know why you want to go on this powerful journey and leave an impact with your work, you need to get clear on your personal vision. Your purpose statement clarified why you want to build your platform. The next chapter will help you crystallize what that platform will look like; that is, the vision you have for the brand you want to build.

CHAPTER 3

Your Vision

Now that you know some of the main mindset shifts needed to follow the Power Your Research method and have your purpose statement, you need to get clear on what amplifying your platform means for you. Your vision, in this context, means understanding what amplifying your platform looks like for you. In essence, **what do you see when you envision the way you want your brand to look six months from now, a year from now, and even five years from now?** What platforms do you want to appear on? What do you want to speak about consistently? By narrowing down where you see yourself appearing in the public sphere as a thought leader, you're being intentional about creating your personal vision for your brand.

The idea here is that once you know what you feel comfortable and excited talking about, you will then be able to move to the next question, which is to identify where you want to be talking about those things. This is because if you do not have a clear goal for what amplifying your platform looks like and where you want to appear, then you cannot successfully measure the success of the Power Your Research method in relation to your own goals. You also will not know when you have reached the vision you set out for yourself because you do not have a clear metric on what that will look like when you see it.

WHAT KEY ITEMS OR ISSUES DO YOU WANT TO TALK ABOUT IN THE MEDIA?

At this stage, it is critical for you to get clear on the keywords you want other people to associate with your name. The process of figuring out what you want to talk about in the media involves answering these two questions:

1. What can you see yourself talking about over and over again?
2. What keywords or phrases do you want to be known for?

Write Down Your Areas of Interest

For the first question, you want to start with your area of research expertise and/or passion.

Take a moment to write out a list of three or four areas you know you have the expertise and passion to talk about consistently. Make sure these areas cover topics you want to speak about in the media and would feel comfortable speaking about today, tomorrow, and years down the line. In other words, would you be happy talking about the same things in five years that you are talking about today?

Do not simply include an area just because the media has asked you to speak about that topic in the past unless it meets the criteria discussed in this section. Be honest with yourself. Building a brand largely involves talking about the same set of topics over an extended period of time so that people begin to associate you with that subject matter. **If you aren't consistent, you cannot build that brand association.**

This list of what you know you can talk about and what you're passionate discussing is critical because you do not want to make the mistake of talking about what you think the media wants you to discuss, as opposed to what is right for you. It will help you be intentional about the media spots you appear on, and it will help you filter out media opportunities that do not make sense for your brand. Without this clarity, you might find yourself going viral for something that you do not want to be known for or associated with.

A Cautionary Tale

I have a friend, we will call her Kim, who came to me because she went on an international news show to talk about COVID-19 when her area of interest and research was accounting. This particular show was looking for hot takes on the vaccine, and they wanted a professor to talk about why they didn't want to get vaccinated. Kim called me to tell me that she went viral for this and that it wasn't what she wanted. This happened because Kim wasn't intentional about her brand positioning. She appeared on the show because she was asked to, and being on an international news show is exciting; however, it isn't always in your best interest. Now Kim has to live with that segment out in the public for the rest of her life. Her university even had questions about the segment. This is not a situation you want to find yourself in, and it can be avoided by getting clear on what you want to talk about in the media.

Just because the media asks, you don't have to accept the invitation if it isn't going to paint you in a positive light. This acts as a filter when media outlets reach out to you to appear on their programs.

This doesn't mean you can only talk about one thing; it means **you want to know your boundaries in terms of what you feel comfortable and excited talking about.**

Writing Down Keywords

The second part of this vision process is coming up with keywords and phrases that you want associated with your name or brand. Why do you need these? When someone types these keywords or terms into Google, you want your name to come up on the first or second page. The talking points list you just created helps you with this.

For example, my dissertation was on the history of Black comic strips, and that was published in 2010. Since then, I have done so many interviews on Black comics and published so many articles and books on the topic that people in the comics industry associate me with Black comics. This is because that phrase is connected to my name based on all of the media content out there over the last fifteen years.

This is the same result you are seeking to achieve through the Power Your Research method. This introductory step of answering these two questions gives you the grounding to be intentional about how your name and work are connected to appropriate phrases. The final section of this chapter is about identifying which outlets you want to appear on.

An Example: Keywords and Phrases

A client, whom I have named Jen, has expertise in the areas of diversity, equity, and inclusion (DEI) as it relates to family mental health. Her list might look like this:

- DEI and mental health
- DEI and the Black family
- DEI, mental health, and Black youth

Jen now knows that going forward, she will be seeking out media spots that are open to these topics, and she knows that she will always say yes to media outlets that reach out to talk about these things.

If Jen were to be asked by the media to talk about DEI and arts administration, she should say no to that outlet. This is because art administration is a very specific field that she does not have knowledge in. As a result, appearing on a show with that topic would result in stress for this client because she is not historically trained in arts administration. Speaking on this topic would dilute her brand and make her uncomfortable when trying to answer the interviewer's questions—and the audience can feel when someone is not comfortable. These are all negative outcomes.

This does not mean that you cannot talk about anything outside your list if asked. It means that, overall, you should create a parameter of topics you will speak on publicly. You want to use your own discernment to make sure anything outside of that parameter is in line with your vision. This focus will help you later on in the process when we begin the work of pitching media outlets.

My Story

Early on in my brand-building journey, I would say yes to any and every media outlet that wanted me to talk to them. It didn't matter if it was an obscure podcast or the *Washington Post*. I was on a quest to get my work out there; however, that put me in some very high-stress and compromising situations that had a negative impact on my brand and what I was trying to do in the world.

When I showed up to talk about subjects I wasn't really an expert in or comfortable talking about, I would stress myself out in the days and hours before the interview scrambling to look up information before airing. Then, after the interview, I would beat myself up because I knew I wasn't confident with the information I'd presented to the public.

You want to avoid all of this by getting clear on your list of topics, seeking media spots that are appropriate for your knowledge base, and then only accepting media invites that are in line with your area(s) of expertise.

WHAT OUTLETS (MEDIA PLACEMENTS) DO YOU WANT TO APPEAR ON?

Now that you know the areas you want to speak on in the media and the keywords you want to be associated with your name, you can identify aligned media outlets. To figure out which outlets you prefer to appear on, you want to do the following three things:

1. Write a dream list of high-level media outlets.
2. Narrow down that list.
3. Write a list of local outlets that align with the first two items.

We will address each one of these in turn, as this is the order in which you should create your media outlets list. Keep in mind that this is your vision for your brand. This is all about where you want to appear, not where someone else has or has not appeared. Sometimes we might think we want to appear in places simply because we have seen a peer on that show, but I want you to make sure that is actually what *you* want.

High-Level Media Outlets

We have all listened to or watched shows, podcasts, and interviews where we felt we could have been the guest or even done a better job than the guest who was interviewed. Have you ever had that feeling? If so, which media outlet was that on? Use this as a springboard to **write down all of the places you'd love to appear.** Do not limit yourself here. Think big, as shooting for the stars results in amazing things happening when it comes to media placements.

These are typically high-level outlets, but they can also be more obscure ones that are specific to your niche. For example, whatever your area of expertise, you might want to appear on these popular networks:

- BBC
- NPR
- ABC
- PBS

Everyone knows these networks, as they are international names recognized around the world.

Narrow It Down

Within those networks you've listed (as well as within your subject area), there are specific magazines, TV shows, programs, and podcasts that will allow you to better position yourself. Therefore, next, you need to get specific within that list.

Keep in mind that if you have already written down a particular program on your list, that's great. Here you just want to get as specific as possible if you haven't already done so.

This also might take a little bit of research on your part to find the exact opportunities within these networks. You should also use this process to ensure it makes sense to be on these outlets.

Here are some questions to ask yourself.

- *Do these outlets even have a program that is friendly to your area of expertise?*
- *Would it even make sense for you to be featured in that outlet? Why would it make sense for that outlet's audience?*

For example, on an early media list, I'd included MSNBC and CNN, with specific shows such as Rachel Maddow and Joy Reid. I wanted to appear on those outlets because I had seen other academics on them; however, I don't do work in the area of politics, and if I am being honest with myself, it would be uncomfortable for me to talk about the ins and outs of the political system in a public forum even if it were related to comics. There isn't a specific show on these networks that would make sense for me.

Use this as an opportunity to get clear and honest with yourself. Keep in mind that if, for example, the Joy Reid show asked me to talk about the latest *Black Panther* movie, I would absolutely say yes because that is my specific area of interest, and it would make sense. However, if her show asked me to connect it to the latest political issue, I'd have to decline the offer. Her show does not often talk about characters like Black Panther or Wonder Woman, and if she invited me to her show to talk about COVID-19, my answer should be an unequivocal no.

An Example: Narrow Down Your Dream List

I have a client who does work on urban development at the intersection of hip-hop and politics. If this client were narrowing down his dream list of media placements, he might write:

- MSNBC → Ari Melber show
- NPR → *Louder Than a Riot*

These specific shows on these networks have a history of talking about hip-hop and politics as well as urban issues.

Niche Programs

At this stage, you also want to include specific niche programs and podcasts that make sense for your brand. For example, I might add these specific podcasts and shows to my hip-hop and politics client's list:

- *The Breakfast Club*
- *Earn Your Leisure*

These podcasts have large followings but are specific to my client's area of interest. If you are not into hip-hop, you likely do not know what those podcasts are. If you are into hip-hop, those podcasts are very popular. That's the point. Choose specific outlets that will get you in front of your specific audience.

When you finish with your broad list and then your narrowed-down list, you will have a very focused listing of a range of ideal media outlets that you can set your sights on and niche outlets that are very reasonable for you to appear on. Later on in the process, when you learn how to pitch media outlets, you will be able to position yourself to land on these outlets.

Going Local

Now, you want to make a final list of the local outlets *that will best position you* to appear on the outlets you have identified so far. What I mean by local outlets are media opportunities in your hometown or home city or a geographical location you have a connection to.

At this stage, you are just getting clear on where you want to appear. Your local list of media outlets will help you build a track record of media spots that are more accessible, so when it is time to pitch yourself to the major outlets you've identified, you will be better aligned to get a favorable response. In other words, local outlets often lead to larger media opportunities.

Where to Look

Nearly every geographical area has its own NPR station. Where I live in Philadelphia, it's called WHYY. Your local outlets typically love regional stories and local professors who are doing great work. They are eager to speak with you and interview you. You also have local newspapers and podcasts that are based in your hometown and city.

Research and make a list of those local outlets. **This list does not need to have a track record of covering stories similar to your field of interest, because local media is typically more open and willing to feature someone who lives in the immediate area.** For example, my local list in Philadelphia might include the following small newspapers and outlets:

- WHYY
- *Southwest Globe Times*
- The *Philadelphia Tribune*
- *Philadelphia Inquirer*
- The *Trentonian*

I also included an outlet (the *Trentonian*) in a neighboring state, New Jersey. You should not be afraid to add neighboring areas to your list.

At this point, combining your three lists, you should have one pretty long list of local outlets and larger national media spots that are a part of your platform expansion. You should shoot for at least fifty outlets between all of your lists, from high level to niche to local. **This is essentially the vision you have for your brand media placements.** (When we move to pitch media later on in the book, you want to start with pitching local, and as you have success, you then move to pitch the larger outlets.)

The fun part about this technique is that as you follow the Power Your Research process, you will get invited to appear in the media on outlets outside of your list as well as outlets that are on your list, as long as they align with your topic areas of expertise. The successes will come more quickly than you expect as you follow this process.

Finally, do not be afraid to think creatively about your list. You can also consider other factors such as the audience of a particular platform, even if that platform doesn't specifically cater to your topic. You can do this as long as you are clear about what you are willing to talk about.

For example, I mentioned a client who does work in the discipline of DEI and mental health. That client might have *The Breakfast Club* on her list of shows. This is a show about hip-hop, so on its face it doesn't look like a place for a scholar who does work in her specific field. However, the audience of *The Breakfast Club* consists predominantly of Black adults between the ages of twenty and forty-five, and because of that, there is an overlap in what they care about. That age range might have kids at home and perhaps more family, so we know they care about the larger issue of mental health. Since this client has clarity from the previous steps we've covered, she can appear on those

This chapter was about getting clarity on your own personal vision for what amplifying your platform means for you. You now have that clarity on what you want to talk about in the media and even where you want to be talking about it. We covered the area(s) of expertise you feel comfortable discussing on a consistent basis and the importance of thinking creatively about the outlets you should appear on or need to appear on. You have taken the time to create a list of a range of media placements that feel right for you as well as niche and local outlets that are a good fit.

Of course, there will be work ahead in order to reach these placements, but knowing the goal will help you navigate this process effectively so you ensure that you make the best media placement decisions for your brand along the way to achieving your goals.

This clarity work will help you identify your brand statement, brand adjectives, and brand archetype—which are the bridges between your vision and how you show up in the real world to position yourself to land those media spots and visibility. As such, the next chapter will cover how to get the clarity you need around messaging and articulating that messaging through identifying your brand assets.

CHAPTER 4

Brand Assets

When you think about brand assets, you probably conjure up ideas for logos, color schemes, and your brand's unique font. While those are part of a personal brand identity, they are not the first elements you need to focus on when it comes to building your brand. Sure, they are important, but they are also cosmetic, and first you need to be clear on who you will show up as in the public sphere. That is, you need to develop a filter through which your brand will operate. You can worry about logos, color schemes, and your brand's unique font once you understand what your brand persona is, what your brand messaging is, and what your brand promise is.

In this chapter, you will do three things:

1. Create your brand statement
2. Identify your brand archetype
3. Identify your brand adjectives

These three core brand assets are what you need to implement an effective social media strategy and to create an emotional connection with your audience, which we cover in the Connection phase of the Power Your Research process.

We will start with your brand statement, because that is the anchor for your brand archetype and brand adjectives. **Your brand statement helps clarify your mission, vision, and purpose as well as your brand's promise.** Your brand statement also helps you clarify the purpose of your research as an academic and why you do the work you do. This is especially important for academics who are used to talking to other academics in technical jargon and three-syllable words.

After identifying your brand statement, we will move on to **identifying your brand archetype, which will give you insight on connecting your brand statement to your brand's messaging.** Many academics struggle with translating their work for a mass audience outside of academia. Your brand archetype will **clarify your brand's personality type and how it represents your brand's characteristics, values, and behaviors.** It helps create a deeper emotional connection between you and your audience, making your work relatable, memorable, and differentiated.

Finally, we will identify **your brand adjectives, which are the lenses through which you post on social media.** This is reserved for last because once you are clear on your brand statement and brand archetype, it makes it easier to identify your brand adjectives. This process will allow all of your brand assets to be in alignment with your mission, vision, and purpose, thus making it easier to translate your academic work for a less academic audience. It will also give you the clarity you need to confidently position yourself outside of academia so that you can better connect with people.

YOUR BRAND STATEMENT

Your brand statement is a critical component of your mission, vision, and purpose. This statement helps you articulate who you are, what you do, and who you do it for. Many academics and educators haven't developed a brand statement, which can contribute to confusion about what they should be posting on social media or even what interests they should pursue. **Your brand statement acts as a North Star, guiding your decision-making and capturing who you are as a professional.** It can help you clarify your direction, plan what you want to work toward, and communicate with your audience. As an academic who can be pulled in so many different directions, it also helps you say yes or no to opportunities. When you are not clear on who you are, who you serve, and why you serve them, you can find yourself saying yes to distractions because you do not have a filter that allows you to see those things as distractions.

Once you have a brand statement, you ask yourself one question when presented with a new opportunity: *Does this opportunity align with my brand statement?* If the answer is no, then it is a distraction, not an opportunity. (See the story about Kim on page 43.)

What Is a Brand Statement?

A brand statement is a personalized expression that defines who you are as a professional, who you help, and how you help them. It should be seen as an essential tool for any educator who shapes how their brand is perceived by peers and potential clients. Not only does this aid in marketing materials and social media posts but also in creating a brand persona across all platforms.

In addition, you can think of your brand statement as a promise to your audience. When your audience engages with your content on LinkedIn, YouTube, X, or even at in-person events, they expect you to adhere to your brand. **This consistency is what builds the trust people need to connect with you on a deeper level.** Your statement will encapsulate your promise and communicate it in as little as one sentence. Here's my brand statement, with bold text for what we will cover:

"I create **experiences** for **free thinkers** to feel **empowered** when they're **challenging the status quo.**"

In only a few seconds, you understand who I am, what I do, and who I do it for. It is clear, yet it also serves as a broad umbrella at the same time. This brand statement captures what I seek to do with Power Your Research all the way to what I seek to do when I write Black Panther and Wonder Woman for places like DC and Marvel comics. This statement is the common thread that connects all of my brand's products and services.

THE FOUR-PART BRAND STATEMENT FORMULA

Because so much of your brand identity will be captured by just one sentence, it's easy to feel overwhelmed when creating your unique statement. It's important to remember that you're unlikely to create the perfect brand statement on your first try. Often, people will perform many revisions and have many one-on-one coaching calls with me before arriving at a statement that defines their brand. So, do not feel bad if it takes you a few tries or if you have to revisit your statement over an extended period of time, tweaking it here and there until you are satisfied. At the same time, you do not want to overthink the brand statement to the point where it acts as a roadblock in moving forward through this process.

So, let's look at how you can create your brand statement. To help you arrive at your statement successfully, I've detailed a four-part brand statement formula. This is a formula I learned from the creative co-working space, REC Philly, that I am currently a member of.

1. I Create _____

The first part of your brand statement defines what you do. You can start this portion by writing "I create _____." As challenging as it is, limit yourself to placing only one word in the blank space. The word you choose should capture what you do while giving you room to grow. Looking at my statement, I said, "I create experiences." Whether I'm running my Power Your Research company, writing for clients, or working on comic books, I'm creating experiences. **In other words, I'm on-brand.**

Here are some examples of what you might include:

- I create content.
- I create audio.
- I create visuals.
- I create spaces.
- I create experiences.
- I create videos.

As you brainstorm your word, avoid using a term like "research." Creating research is standard for most academics, so not only does this word fail to distinguish you from other education professionals, but it's also limiting. You'll likely do much more than create research in the future. Starting your statement with this could fail to encapsulate your whole brand and future endeavors. Many people reading this book are multi-passionate academics.

2. I Create _____ for_____ _____

The second part of your brand statement communicates whom you create for. Think about who you want to engage with and limit this fill-in-the-blank to two words: an adjective and a noun. You want these words to be descriptive. Try to avoid using demographics like age, race, or religion. According to Jim Joseph from entrepreneur.com, even in-depth demographic descriptions can only paint a limited picture of your audience. Demographics can mislead your brand direction because there isn't enough information to guide brand positioning accurately. You want to lean more into the *psychographics* of the people you want to reach.

Psychographics are different from demographics in that they focus on the attitudes and behaviors of people rather than their age, gender, or income level. This allows marketers to gain a deeper understanding of their target audience and create campaigns that resonate with them on an emotional level. With psychographics, marketers can craft messages that speak directly to their customers' needs and wants.

My statement says, "I create experiences for **free thinkers**." I chose "free thinkers" because people who engage with my content must think outside the box. They're people who challenge their limiting self-beliefs. I am pretty sure that if you're reading this book, you in some way identify as a free thinker or aspire to be one. That is what my content attracts, whether I am selling comic books or branding courses. I am on-brand for my audience.

3. I Create _____ for_____ _____ to Feel _____

The third section of your brand statement explains what you want your audience to feel. Limit yourself to one word for this section as well. I want my free thinkers to feel empowered when they engage with my content, so my word is "empowered." It used to be "inspired," but I changed it because "empowered" captured the feeling I aim for more accurately.

Here are some examples of words you might choose:

- Engaged
- Eager
- Accepted
- Inspired

4. I Create _____ for_____ _____ to Feel _____ When They're _____.

The last of the four sections in your brand statement describes **when** your audience should experience the feeling you're trying to evoke.

That means I want my free thinkers to experience empowerment when they're challenging the status quo. The status quo could represent a range of things, from a relationship to higher education. Regardless of the status quo for an individual, I want them to feel empowered when they're actively challenging it.

Once you complete this final section, you will have a working brand statement. Remember, your brand statement may change over time, just like mine did, but you shouldn't obsess over it or revise it too often. Do not overthink this.

Using Your Brand Statement

Brand statements can be used in a variety of places to help educators and academics create their online persona and navigate digital spaces, make important career-related decisions, and stay on the professional track they've set.

Ultimately, strategically using your brand statement can help you to always project a consistent professional image. Because of the internal clarity your brand statement brings you, it is most useful in two critical areas of brand building.

Social Media

A brand statement can be a valuable tool for educators and academics engaging with social media. It serves as a guide for the kinds of content you should and shouldn't post, helping to keep posts on-brand. It will also remind you to think about how you want your audience to interact with your brand so that when they comment or engage with your content, it aligns with your brand's values. This can have a major impact on the kind of interactions you have, as well as how your audience responds to what you post.

Decision-Making

As an academic or educator, your brand statement is key to making important decisions, as it can help you determine where to focus your attention and energy, which then affects your existing schedule and how you manage your time. Your brand statement is deeply connected to your purpose statement, which captures the impact you seek to have on the world.

An Example: How These Brand Assets Work Together

Here is an example of how one's brand statement and "why" statement work together from one of my clients, whom we will call Tasha. For context, Tasha said she wanted to appear on media outlets that allow her to talk about challenging the publishing industry in terms of making it more diverse.

Excerpt from Tasha's Why Statement

My mother always wanted to be a published writer but didn't have the access or resources. As someone who is published, I am committed to reaching my goals because my mother didn't live long enough to see me break barriers as a writer. I am committed to my success because I want to make her proud and ensure that my nephews have opportunities no one in our family did.

Tasha's Brand Statement

I create content for creative writers to feel supported when they're breaking barriers in publishing.

As you can see, there is continuity between Tasha's purpose and her brand statement. You should strive for this as well. While you are doing this work, it might not always align perfectly right away, but you want to think strategically about aligning these aspects because this will serve you in communicating clearly to your audience later on.

YOUR BRAND ARCHETYPE

Before discussing brand archetypes in depth, it's important to understand a few key points. First, there is no objective test or diagnostic that can determine your brand archetype. Second, this is not a section you want to get stuck on in terms of trying to pick "the perfect" brand archetype, because you can always come back and change it later. Finally, it is likely that after learning about all twelve brand archetypes, you will like a few of them. Your job is to choose one and move on without overthinking your selection. You can always revisit your choice down the line, and you might even need to as you learn more about the audience you are trying to reach. These three disclaimers are what I tell all of my clients before going over the brand archetypes in order to temper expectations and alleviate any nervousness in choosing the "right" one.

As academics, we like to have a clear formula and path, yet much of the work of building your brand is not a $1 + 1 = 2$ formula. This is especially true for this section. As you embark on this journey, you will discover that there is discernment, logic, and trial and error involved as unique situations occur. This is important to understand because this brand archetype section is relatively brief, as I could dedicate an entire book to this subject. This section will cover the following:

1. What a brand archetype is and how you can use it
2. A brief explanation of each brand archetype, along with goals and examples
3. How to choose your brand archetype

Each brand archetype will begin by stating the archetype's goal, as my clients have found it helpful to know the motivations of each brand archetype when trying to select their own. If the goal of the archetype feels in alignment with your personality and mission, it might be one you want to consider for yourself.

What Is a Brand Archetype?

A brand archetype is a symbolic personality that represents a brand and influences how the brand communicates and behaves. The concept of archetypes was popularized by the Swiss psychologist Carl Jung, who believed that archetypes are universal, symbolic patterns that exist in the collective unconscious of all human beings. Jung is best known for his pioneering work in the field of analytical psychology. Jung's theory of psychological types was based on the idea that people differ in their preferences and attitudes. However, they all have one dominant trait that steers them toward typical behavioral patterns, motivations, values, and desires. He dubbed these "personality archetypes." These personality types are what brands can use to communicate their identity, mission, values, and goals.

As you read the descriptions and examples of the brand archetypes, write down the ones that feel most in line with who you are in terms of personality, goals, motivations, and the audience you want to reach. I also encourage you to do outside research on these archetypes to get additional examples and ideas.

Using a particular brand archetype can allow a business to create a personality of its own that can better relate to its target demographic and psychographics on a personal and emotional level. When building a personal brand in the business world, individuals can use archetypes to distinguish themselves from their competitors. Having an archetype—certain behavior patterns, traits, or values—that your ideal audience can align with helps you become recognizable.

Since you are clear on your brand statement, and you know who you are creating for, you now are perfectly set up to better understand how to communicate with your audience with a consistent tone and feel. Your archetype will help you do that. While we haven't reached the stage of the process where you know far-reaching details about your audience, at this point you are taking an educated guess about the type of people you want to reach and the messaging you want to share with them.

For example, in Tasha's brand statement (page 60), she knows her target audience is "creative writers," but that doesn't tell us much about the actual people she will be interacting with online and in person. Your brand archetype will get you closer to crafting your messaging strategy and your brand's mission for that target audience, and as you move forward through this process, you'll learn more techniques to really get to know who the people are that you are serving.

In short, your brand archetype will bring you closer to understanding the goal of your research/area of expertise as it relates to how you communicate with your ideal audience. As such, you can use the archetype as a guide for developing your visual and verbal communication style, messaging, and behaviors.

By aligning your personal brand with a specific archetype, you can create a clear and consistent brand personality that is authentic and resonates with your target audience as well you and your own personality. Let's dive into Jung's twelve archetypes. As mentioned, while reading about these archetypes, jot down notes on the three or four that feel most in alignment with who you are. After that, I will help you narrow your list down to one.

The Twelve Brand Archetypes: Explanation and Examples

Brands use archetypes to help build a narrative and to create an emotional connection with their target audience. Your brand archetype will give you the clarity you need to connect with the people who care about the things you care about. As we go through the twelve brand arche-types, please note that the application of these archetypes as they relate to specific people and brands are based on my research and analysis of the brands I am associating them with as well as research conducted for this book. I am in no way claiming that these people and organizations abide by the parameters of these archetypes or have publicly stated that they indeed follow the messaging of these brands.

The Innocent Child

The goal of the Innocent Child brand archetype is to maintain opti-mism, simplicity, and happiness. If these goals feel compatible with your personality, this archetype might be in alignment with who you are and what your audience needs. The Innocent Child is also known as the "dreamer" or "idealist," and it portrays lightheartedness, open-mindedness, and happiness. Campaigns based on this archetype may convey nostalgic, minimalist, or vintage aesthetics as a way of appealing to one's inner Innocent Child.

Fred Rogers, who earned degrees in music composition and divin-ity, is best known for his children's television program *Mister Rogers' Neighborhood*. His persona is best exemplified by the Innocent Child, as he created a nurturing and safe space for children to learn and explore. He spoke directly to children in a calm and gentle voice, wear-ing simple and unassuming clothing, and he often incorporated songs, puppets, and other childlike elements into his show.[9]

Rogers' Innocent Child archetype helped him connect with chil-dren and parents alike, and his program is still a beloved childhood memory for many. According to Know Your Archetypes online, other real-life people associated with the Innocent Child include Dolly Par-ton and Shirley Temple.[10]

The Orphan or the Everyman

The goal of the Orphan (also referred to as the Everyman) brand arche-type is to create connection and a sense of belonging. It's massively effective in reaching customers because everyone has an "orphan" inside of them. This archetype is shaped by abandonment, neglect, and nonbelonging, and branding will tell a campaign story through this lens. You likely know this archetype in literature—think Harry Potter or Batman. But what about well-known personal brands? Most brands are unlikely to take the Orphan archetype at face value. They're more likely to design a powerful character arc like one in which the Orphan becomes the Hero (just like in *Harry Potter* and *Batman*).

Brené Brown, who holds a PhD in social work and is a research pro-fessor at the University of Houston, is known for her work on vulnerabil-ity, shame, and empathy. Her brand archetype exemplifies the Orphan, which she uses to connect with her audience on a deep emotional level. As you can see in the image below, she often posts images on Instagram that communicate connection and belonging in different ways.

Brown often talks about her own struggles with vulnerability and shame, and how she has learned to overcome them. By sharing her personal stories and experiences, she creates a sense of empathy and relatability with her audience, making them feel understood and less alone in their own struggles. As Brown's post on the previous page demonstrates, if this archetype is shaped by abandonment, neglect, and nonbelonging, her content shows people how to love each other and how to love themselves so they can feel connected.

Brown's use of the Orphan archetype has helped her become a best-selling author, a TED speaker, and a leading authority in her field. She has inspired countless people around the world to embrace vulnerability and lead more authentic and fulfilling lives.[11]

The Hero

The Hero brand archetype is characterized by a strong desire to achieve a specific goal or mission, often involving overcoming obstacles and challenges. Brand strategists favor the Hero because it's powerful and inspiring. You'll often see this messaging used for brands in sportswear, emergency utility services, outdoor equipment, and so on. Any individual who seeks to serve others, is committed to achievement, or prioritizes duty as one of their convictions will favor the Hero in its branding.

MrBeast, a popular YouTube creator and influencer, exemplifies the Hero. He displays the Hero traits of being both a powerful and inspiring presence as he hosts online challenges and stunts that almost always have a donation component for individuals who need financial assistance.

Angela Duckworth is a psychologist and a professor of psychology at the University of Pennsylvania. She is best known for her research on grit, which she defines as a combination of passion and perseverance toward long-term goals.

Duckworth's brand archetype represents the Hero, which she uses to inspire and motivate her audience to overcome obstacles and achieve their goals. She often speaks about her own struggles with self-doubt and failure, and how she used grit to persevere and succeed (to become her own hero). By sharing her personal stories and insights, she creates a sense of admiration and respect among her audience, making them feel empowered and motivated to pursue their own dreams.

Duckworth argues that while talent and intelligence are important for success, they are not enough. Grit is what separates those who achieve their goals from those who do not. She suggests that grit can be developed and cultivated, and that it is particularly important in challenging situations where success is not guaranteed.

Duckworth's use of the Hero archetype has helped her become a best-selling author, a TED speaker, and a recognized authority in her field, and she has inspired countless people to develop grit and resilience in their own lives.[12] Or to become the heroes of their own story.

The Explorer

The goal of the Explorer brand archetype is to seek new experiences and discover the world. The Explorer—as you might expect—wants to go to places less traveled. This archetype is all about feeling that rush of adrenaline that comes with continual movement. This brand places value on autonomy and individualism while simultaneously encouraging self-discovery. Unlike the Hero, however, the Explorer isn't about winning or proving its worth. It's just about being free and daring.

Jane Goodall is a British primatologist, anthropologist, and UN Messenger of Peace, best known for her groundbreaking research on chimpanzees, and she is a great example of this archetype. She promotes environmental conservation and inspires curiosity and wonder about the natural world.[13]

Goodall's research on chimpanzees revolutionized our understanding of animal behavior and the close evolutionary relationship between humans and primates. She has spent more than fifty years studying and advocating for the conservation of chimpanzees and their habitats and has inspired generations of scientists and nature enthusiasts to explore and appreciate the natural world.

Goodall's use of the Explorer archetype has helped her become a best-selling author, a TED speaker, and a leading advocate for animal welfare and environmental conservation.

Another example of the Explorer is Jesse Itzler, an entrepreneur, author, and rapper. Itzler is the cofounder of Marquis Jet, one of the largest private jet card companies. (He is also the husband of Sara Blakely, founder and owner of Spanx.)

Itzler's social media is characterized by a desire to seek out new experiences, take risks, and live life to the fullest. Not only that, but his entrepreneurial ventures reflect his desire to explore new opportunities and push boundaries. He has even written a book, *Living with a SEAL*, about his experience inviting a Navy SEAL to live with him for a month to push him to his limits both physically and mentally. Below is an example of the type of content Itzler pushes out on his social media pages:

"If you do everything in moderation, you will live a moderate life. Not what I signed up for!"

- @jesseitzler

jesseitzler ⚬

jesseitzler ⚬ Show me one top CEO, one NBA player, one best selling author, one Oscar winner, one Olympic gold medalist, one ground breaking entrepreneur, one Broadway dancer, one ultra-runner, etc....that got there with moderation.

I'll wait.

Edited · 63w

Liked by   and 5,267 others
MAY 13, 2022

Add a comment...

The Caregiver

The goal of the Caregiver is to care for and protect others. The Caregiver is one of the easiest brand archetypes to place. It's often found in nurturing careers (think healthcare or nonprofit organizations). Brands that use this archetype will highlight real-world problems while simultaneously seeking to evoke feelings of sentimentality and familial devotion. Common features in advertising include images of family or the community as well as touching music.

According to Know Your Archetypes online, key examples of the Caregiver are individuals like Princess Diana and Nelson Mandela, who built their persona on selflessness. They devoted their time and energy to looking after others, and they were beloved because of that. In addition, Paul Farmer was a medical anthropologist and physician who dedicated his career to providing healthcare to some of the world's most vulnerable populations.[14] His brand archetype was an example of the Caregiver, which he used to emphasize the importance of empathy and compassion in healthcare and social justice.

Farmer cofounded Partners In Health, a nonprofit organization that provides healthcare to people in impoverished communities around the world. He spent much of his career working in Haiti, where he helped establish a network of health clinics and hospitals, serving hundreds of thousands of people. As you can see in the Instagram post on the next page, Farmer's team continues to exemplify the Caregiver archetype by embodying compassion, empathy, and a deep sense of responsibility to those in need. They work tirelessly to provide healthcare services to those who would otherwise go without, and they are driven by a deep commitment to social justice and equity. PIH serves as a powerful testament to the transformative power of compassion and selflessness in healthcare.

The Rebel or the Outlaw

The goal of the Rebel (also referred to as the Outlaw) is to break the rules and challenge the status quo. A brand using the Rebel archetype conveys a disruptive force. It may seek to be disruptive for its own purposes or because it can improve the lives of others by bursting through current boundaries. While rebels are outside of the norm, they inspire change and a deviation from the status quo (for the better).

A great example of a brand using the Rebel archetype is Apple. Apple shows how they're pushing limits in the current market. Steve Jobs designed the iPhone because he wanted a phone that had internet capability, an MP3 player, and a two-megapixel digital camera—something that other brands weren't even thinking about yet. He was a rebel in the tech industry.

Cornel West is a philosopher, political activist, and author known for his provocative and controversial views on race, politics, and society. His brand archetype is an example of the Rebel, which he uses to challenge mainstream ideas and promote social justice and equality. West's work spans a wide range of topics, including African American history, democracy, religion, and Marxism. He is known for his critiques of capitalism and neoliberalism and his advocacy for socialism and anti-racism. West's use of the Rebel archetype has helped him become a prominent public intellectual and activist, with a large following among students, academics, and activists. He has written numerous books, articles, and essays, and is a frequent commentator in the media on issues related to race, politics, and society.

Look at the Instagram post from the CEO of Black Girl Ventures, whose brand exemplifies the Rebel by disrupting the venture capital business.

Serial entrepreneur and computer scientist Shelly Bell's social media content and her messaging on the platforms she appears on are all about disruption within the context of funding. She founded Black Girl Ventures in response to the systemic barriers faced by Black and Brown women entrepreneurs in accessing capital and other resources. Through BGV, Bell has created a platform that challenges the status quo and empowers women of color to take control of their own destinies.

The Creator

The goal of the Creator is to bring ideas and visions to life. The Creator is a common path for brands in the marketing, technology, or design fields. Many of my clients who are professors of design or interior design naturally lean toward this archetype. If your business is creating something—anything—new, then you can use this archetype to your advantage in branding. If you're marketing yourself as a Creator, you'll want to showcase highly aesthetic and polished products that inspire people to engage in the creative process themselves.

Two great examples of Creators in branding include Crayola and YouTube. Crayola's products appeal to every age with their slogans like "The Power of Creativity—Crayola—It Starts Here." They remind consumers that they create products that can unleash creativity and originality. YouTube fosters the creation of new ideas through open expression. It's even dubbed its video makers "Creators."

However, if you're interested in building a personal brand more specific to an individual than a company, look at Martha Stewart or Tim Burton. These individuals put a lot of value into the creative process, and as a result, they spend lots of time on single projects to ensure perfection. In addition, Neil deGrasse Tyson is an astrophysicist, author, and science communicator who has become one of the most recognizable figures in popular science.[15] His brand archetype is a great example of the Creator, which he uses to emphasize the importance of curiosity, imagination, and creativity in science and education. As you can see in the Instagram post on the next page, Tyson does a great job of bringing people into the world of science through creativity and imagination. In the Instagram post, he is doing just that by using the popular TV show *Star Trek* to generate interest in his own show, *Nova ScienceNOW.*

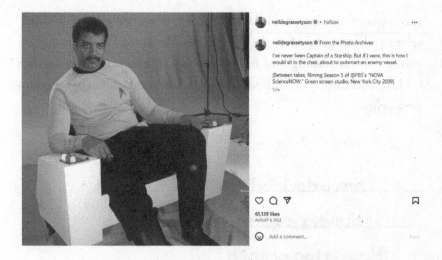

Tyson's work spans a wide range of topics, including the origins of the universe, the search for extraterrestrial life, and the importance of science literacy. He is known for his ability to communicate complex scientific concepts in an engaging and accessible way, as well as for his passion for inspiring a new generation of scientists and thinkers.

Tyson's use of the Creator archetype has helped him become a popular television host, author, and public speaker, with a large following among science enthusiasts as well as the general public. He has hosted several popular television programs, including *Cosmos: A Spacetime Odyssey*, and has written numerous books on science and astrophysics.

The Jester

The goal of the Jester is to entertain and bring joy and humor. As the name suggests, the Jester lights up the world with the joy they bring others. The Jester wants to live in the moment, and they invite everyone around them to do the same. They convey a sense of humor and lightheartedness. At times, they may even come off as mischievous or irreverent.

An example of the Jester archetype is Ellen DeGeneres. She spent years on TV entertaining talk show guests and giving away prizes in the hopes of making people laugh. She wants everyone to enjoy themselves and feel good after she's performed. In all of Ellen's Instagram images, she is smiling and happy. Her social media content focuses on love and displays of kindness, as you can see in Ellen's Instagram post below.

The Sage

My brand archetype is the Sage. The goal of the Sage is to seek and share knowledge and wisdom. Also known as the Scholar, this archetype revolves around truth and knowledge. Sages relentlessly pursue the truth, so they seek out reliable information to share with their consumers. Examples of the Sage include BBC, Google, and PBS. They convey confidence as knowledgeable brands in their field. As a personal brand, the Sage is demonstrated by Oprah, who is widely known and respected as a source of information.

An example of an academic who exemplifies the Sage brand archetype is Noam Chomsky. Chomsky has a PhD in linguistics from the University of Pennsylvania and has been a professor of linguistics at the Massachusetts Institute of Technology for over fifty years. He is known for his contributions to the study of language, as well as for his critiques of power structures and social institutions. His brand archetype represents the Sage because he emphasizes the importance of critical thinking, intellectual rigor, and independent thought. He then shares his findings with others. Chomsky's Instagram page is all about speaking his truth in the name of activism, regardless of the subject matter, as you can see from his post below about climate change:

Chomsky's work spans a wide range of topics, including linguistics, philosophy, and political theory.[16] Beyond his groundbreaking research on the structure of language, which has had a profound impact on the field of linguistics, Chomsky is also known for his outspoken critiques of political and social institutions, particularly those related to power and oppression.

Chomsky's use of the Sage archetype has helped him become one of the most influential public intellectuals of the twentieth and twenty-first centuries, with a large following among academics, activists, and the general public. He has authored over one hundred books and has been a vocal advocate for social justice and human rights throughout his career.

MY ARCHETYPE

When choosing the brand archetype that I would identify with, I initially had a few selected: the Creator, the Rebel, and the Sage. They all resonated with me and felt naturally connected to who I am and what my goals are. However, I ultimately committed to the Sage, not just because it felt more aligned with who I am, but also because of my profession as a professor. The brand archetype you choose may or may not be connected to a job title; however, the motivations, goals, and values that each archetype represents should allow you to feel connected to it, without feeling like it is inauthentic to who you naturally are.

The Ruler

The goal of the Ruler is to lead and take control, creating order and stability. Also known as the Judge, this archetype craves control. Rulers require security and order to both gain and retain power, so they're a stickler for policies. Their priorities include power, status, and organization. Most people associate the Ruler with brands that are classical, noble, and proper. They maximize their consumers' needs to feel safe, empowered, and important.

Anna Wintour—editor-in-chief of *Vogue* since 1988—exemplifies the Ruler archetype. She has a reputation for being icy, scary, and fabulous. She has a powerful presence and uses that demeanor to run the most successful fashion magazine in the world.

Angela Merkel, a German politician who served as the chancellor of Germany from 2005 to 2021, is also an example of the Ruler archetype. Markel has a PhD in quantum chemistry and worked as a research scientist before entering politics.

Merkel projects an image of stability, competence, and authority. This is another example where the brand archetype aligns with the person's profession. Most would agree that the chancellor of Germany is akin to being a "ruler."

Merkel's use of the Ruler archetype has been instrumental in her political success, as she has been able to establish herself as a respected leader both domestically and internationally. Her leadership style is characterized by a focus on pragmatism, consensus building, and long-term planning, which are all consistent with the values of the Ruler archetype. Throughout her tenure as chancellor, Merkel was widely regarded as one of the most powerful women in the world, and her leadership was credited with helping to stabilize the European Union during a period of economic and political turbulence.

The Magician

The goal of the Magician is to transform reality and create something extraordinary. This archetype is for brands that want to deliver transformative experiences. They make their customers' dreams come true. You're probably thinking of a standout example of the Magician right now. One company has made "Where Dreams Come True" their tagline—and they do it so well it's hard to compare anyone else to it. Disney's theme parks are famous for being locations where families can make wishes and experience magic. The adherence to the Magician brand is consistent in its product offerings directed at families.

Carl Sagan, the American astronomer, cosmologist, astrophysicist, astrobiologist, author, and science communicator, had a PhD in astronomy and astrophysics from the University of Chicago.[17] His use of the Magician archetype was evident in his ability to inspire wonder and curiosity in his audiences through his ability to explain complex scientific ideas in a way that was both understandable and captivating.

Sagan's use of the Magician archetype helped establish him as one of the most influential science communicators of the twentieth century. He hosted the television series *Cosmos: A Personal Voyage*, which was widely regarded as a landmark in science communication, and his books, including *The Dragons of Eden* and *Pale Blue Dot*, continue to be widely read and have inspired generations of scientists and science enthusiasts.

The Lover

The goal of the Lover brand archetype is to create a strong emotional connection and to build a committed relationship with people. In addition, the Lover archetype may be the expert teaching others how to build healthier and stronger relationships, thus showing them how to experience more joy, connection, and love. The Lover archetype focuses on feelings of love and passion, and it inspires individuals to seek and experience profound connections in their own lives. The Lover archetype may aim to help people feel attractive and accepted. It is all about helping people experience joy and delight in the context of relationship building. Ultimately, the goal of the Lover is to build a brand or narrative associated with love, desire, and emotional fulfillment.

Stephan Labossiere, also known as Stephan Speaks, is a great example of the Lover brand archetype. I first discovered him on an episode of the Lewis Howes podcast, where he talked extensively about his work as a relationship coach. Labossiere is not only a relationship coach but also a speaker and author who aims to help individuals improve their romantic relationships and find emotional fulfillment. His account provides advice and encouragement around intimacy and partnership. For example, one of his recent X posts has over two thousand likes and says, "Be with someone who will take care of you. Not materialistically, but take care of your soul, well-being, and heart." Stephan Labossiere's work public persona reflects this archetype by promoting emotional intimacy, passionate love, and personal growth within the context of relationships.

Dr. John Gottman is a well-known professor who focuses on healthy relationships and is an example of the Lover archetype. Dr. Gottman is a renowned psychologist, researcher, and author who has dedicated his career to studying relationships and marital stability. He is the cofounder of the Gottman Institute, where he and his team conduct extensive research on couples and relationships. The Gottman Institute's Instagram page is a great example of the consistency of the Lover archetype. Each post is about relationships and connection. Below is an example:

While assessing these twelve archetypes, remember that people are complex and may fit into many of the brand archetypes described; however, to build a successful brand, you need to rely on the consistency of your messaging. You do that by getting clear on one brand archetype and tailoring your messaging and content through that archetype. It is possible that you have read through all twelve brand archetypes and identified one immediately. If that is the case, that's great—you can skip the next section. For most, you will need a method to narrow them down to one. If you fit into the latter category, the next section will help you do that.

How to Determine Your Brand Archetype

Jot down three or four brand archetypes that resonate with your personality and the messaging that might work best for your audience. Now, you need to take that short list and choose just one that resonates with you and your target audience and is also in line with your goals.

For example, if you're an economist and your vision is to disrupt the venture capital space, then you certainly wouldn't choose the Innocent Child or the Jester. These would not help you connect with an audience that is looking for someone who is a disruptor or visionary. An economist looking to disrupt the venture capital space would have to be more of a Rebel in terms of challenging the status quo around how businesses get funded. Or they might want to position themselves as the Hero to the communities they want to serve.

In this example, you'd choose between those two based on your motivations and desires. Or you can think about it this way: if your line of work or expertise inherently reminds you of one of the archetypes, it might be an easy choice for you.

Here are a few ways you can identify your brand archetype if you're starting from square one.

- First, consider your values and mission. These could inherently remind you of one of the archetypes above, or your industry could make your choice easy for you. For example, if you work in a healthcare-related field, the Caregiver is an easy archetype to select.
- Second, think about the emotion you want to convey to your audience. Research shows that an emotional appeal is effective, so putting yourself in the shoes of the people you want to reach and knowing how you want them to feel is essential.
- Finally, consider the audience you're seeking to connect with and the community you're seeking to build. How will they

respond to the archetype in question? Will they connect to it? Answering these questions is a solid start toward identifying your brand archetype and, more importantly, identifying how it will align with your values and the values of your audience.

You want a definite through line between your brand archetype and brand statement. Remember, the brand statement that you created is about the promise you are making to a specific group of people. Therefore, you'll want your archetype to be a good fit for your brand promise to that audience.

For example, the Innocent Child archetype is a brand positioning often associated with children and the innocence of childhood. It is often used in marketing campaigns for products that are targeted toward children, such as Mister Rogers.

Therefore, for illustrative purposes, a brand statement for Mister Rogers might look something like this: "I create experiences for imaginative children to feel curious when they're engaging with their neighborhood."

You can see a clear connection between what the Innocent archetype represents and Mister Rogers' brand promise. This is how you want your brand statement and brand archetype to work together.

As I said earlier, my brand archetype is the Sage. The Sage archetype is seen as wise, knowledgeable, and experienced. They are often seen as the experts in their field. As someone who does coaching and consulting, this is critical to the way I want my audience to perceive me, and if you follow my content online, I represent myself as the expert in my field by showing my history of results and proof of accomplishments. The Sage enjoys seeking knowledge and disseminating that knowledge, which speaks to my values and belief system.

Your brand archetype is not a misrepresentation of who you are; it is, instead, the best representation of you and a part of your brand promise. However, it is also a realistic and true representation of you.

My brand statement works in tandem with my brand archetype to support my goals, values, mission, and vision.

Now that you've identified two out of three of your brand assets, you are well positioned to identify your brand adjectives. The work you have done so far will make the brand adjectives section much easier. Have your brand statement and brand archetype identified before moving on, as each step in the Power Your Research process builds off of the previous step.

WHAT ARE YOUR BRAND ADJECTIVES?

Brand adjectives are words that describe a company's identity and personality. For educators and academics, brand adjectives have the same function, but rather than describing a company, they're used to describe your professional brand as it relates to your personality. This section has been saved for the last part of your brand assets because your brand statement and brand archetype will provide clues as to what your brand adjectives are.

Brand adjectives should be chosen carefully, but I do not want you to get stuck on this part, as you can always go back and tweak the three adjectives you choose. Your brand adjectives are used to show who you are, which then allows you to differentiate yourself in the marketplace. Therefore, they become an integral part of brand communication. The right brand adjectives can help educators and academics connect with their target audiences on a more personal level while building credibility, trust, loyalty, and even professionalism.

Your brand adjectives will help you in these two key areas:

1. Your social media strategy (which we cover in the next chapter)
2. Creating a consistent presence online, which is briefly discussed next

Create a Consistent Presence Online

Using brand adjectives is an effective way to create a consistent presence online. Your brand adjectives are who you will show up as when you turn on your camera to record a video or do speaking engagements. You should show up as your brand adjectives in public because what the audience wants is consistency from the personal brands they follow. For example, you are more likely to follow a certain comedian and become a loyal supporter if their content makes you laugh. If you see them do a stand-up comedy show and they are not funny, you will likely not come to another show or watch any of their specials that air on TV. This is similar to how you should think about your brand adjectives as we go through the upcoming activity to help you identify your own adjectives.

Brand adjectives can emphasize characteristics that deeply resonate with your audience and create powerful imagery that evokes emotion and helps shape how people perceive you. From establishing brand values to communicating with customers and partners, brand adjectives are the perfect way to ensure everyone is on the same page about who you are.

How to Come Up with Three Brand Adjectives: Create Your Own List

Ask yourself, **on my best day, who do I show up as?** Now, create a list of several adjectives, using that question, that reflect who you are, and try to narrow down three from that list. Choose three more closely aligned with who you are and who you want to present as publicly.

This endeavor doesn't have to be complicated. When on coaching calls with clients, I find it most helpful to think about the three characteristics that define them at their very best. From there, we brainstorm a list of words representing those qualities and work to narrow down the list until they come up with the brand adjectives that fit best.

My brand adjectives are: smart, fearless, and empowering.

To help get you started, here are fifteen examples of brand adjectives to inspire you:

• Wise	• Classic	• Visionary
• Happy	• Aspirational	• Warm
• Energized	• Innovative	• Enduring
• Charged	• Reflective	• Generous
• Inclusive	• Spiritual	• Noble

When constructing brand adjectives, consider how they contribute to your overall message. By thoughtfully crafting these brand elements, you can use them consistently in all communications with your audience, creating a unified brand identity on any platform.

BRAND ASSETS IN ACTION

This chapter will conclude with the key takeaways of your three brand assets, how they all work together, and examples from clients who have completed this step.

- Your brand statement is the North Star that guides all your decisions and ensures you stay on track. By now, you have a clear understanding of what a brand statement is and how to create one using the four-part formula covered early in this chapter.
- You've identified the brand archetype that establishes a through line between the elements of your brand statement and your brand persona. Your brand archetype is one of twelve options. This clarifies your brand promise, core desires, goals, and motivations. This helps you understand the proper messaging for your audience as well as the value system that governs your brand persona.

- We've reviewed the importance of having two to three strong brand adjectives that capture the essence of your brand. This makes up who you will show up as online, yet it is also authentic to who you actually are.

Together, your brand statement, brand archetype, and brand adjectives work as part of your **brand identity assets**, which will help define your brand positioning relative to others in your field. These brand identity assets are important across all your communication channels and for your content strategy.

Examples of Brand Assets from Clients

Note: The names used are fictitious in order to protect the confidentiality of clients I have worked with.

Dr. Cindy Prance, a professor in the interior design field
Brand statement: I create tools for radical designers to feel empowered when they're looking to overcome challenges.
Brand archetype: The Creator
Brand adjectives: Thoughtful, creative, strategic

Dr. Cynthia Newland, an academic in the DEI and mental health field
Brand statement: I create resources for visionaries to feel liberated when they're challenging the status quo.
Brand archetype: The Rebel
Brand adjectives: Narrative changer, visionary, trailblazer

Dr. Derek Brent, a professor in the design and leadership field
Brand statement: I create experiences for knowledge seekers to feel fearless when they're building something new.
Brand archetype: The Creator
Brand adjectives: Connector, intelligent, social

Your brand statement, brand archetype, and brand adjectives work together to create a cohesive and compelling personal brand that clarifies and demystifies who you are for yourself and your audience. This is the clarity you need to move on to the next phase in the Power Your Research process: Connection. This is where we will cover developing your social media strategy, getting your ideas to spread, and attracting media coverage and visibility. It's about getting your work in front of a critical mass of the right people so that you can establish a relationship with them.

PART II

Connection

CHAPTER 5

Social Media Strategy

These next few chapters are all about learning how to connect with the community of people who need your help the most. Social media is the best starting place to connect with people, and your social media strategy is a key tool for building and activating your community. In order to get people to engage with you on social media, you need to be passionate about your area of interest, and you need to be consistent. This is why the brand asset work we've already completed is so crucial. This chapter will cover the following:

1. Why socials matter in your brand-building process
2. Implementation of a consistent social media strategy
3. Learning about your audience after implementation
4. The Diffusion of Innovation theory

Remember, you already know what you've promised your target audience (your brand statement). You already know the goals and intent of your content (brand archetype). And you know the three adjectives through which you will filter your content (brand adjectives).

These brand assets position your brand for consistency and clarity in the online sphere. As you read this chapter, keep your brand assets top of mind, as they are the foundation of your social media content.

WHY SOCIALS MATTER IN YOUR BRAND-BUILDING PROCESS

You did the work to create your brand assets; now you need to use them in the real world. This is where your brand identity will be most useful.

In today's digital age, social media platforms have become an integral part of our lives, and leveraging them effectively can help personal brands create a significant impact on their target audience. Social media is a powerful tool that allows brands to reach out to a vast and diverse group of people. With over 4.2 billion active social media users worldwide, it has become the go-to method for brands to showcase their products and services, engage with people, and build a loyal fan base. Social media provides a unique opportunity for brands to engage in direct connection with their target audience and gain valuable insights into their preferences and behaviors. This is key for academics who want to increase their visibility, authority, and income.

Social media platforms such as Facebook, Instagram, TikTok, Threads, X, and LinkedIn provide brands with a global platform to reach out to their target audience, build brand awareness, and establish themselves as industry leaders. By consistently sharing high-quality posts and engaging with followers, brands can create a strong brand image and increase their visibility.

Also, by engaging with followers and responding to their queries and comments, brands can create a sense of community and foster a strong relationship with their audience. This, in turn, can lead to increased brand loyalty, more income opportunities, and positive word-of-mouth marketing.

Another crucial aspect of social media is its ability to provide valuable insights into your communities' behaviors and preferences. By monitoring social media conversations, brands can gain a better understanding of what their target audience wants, how they perceive the brand, and what motivates their decisions.

This information can be used to create more targeted and effective marketing campaigns that resonate with the audience and drive conversions. You'll learn in this chapter that the more you post on social media, the more you will learn how to better tailor your content in the future.

Social media is also an excellent platform for brands to showcase their brand personality and values. Therefore, this is the place where you will be showing up based on your brand assets, which is why we needed to get clear on those in the previous chapters. By creating a consistent brand voice and messaging, you can communicate your values, goals, and personality effectively to your audience. This will help create an emotional connection with people and build strong brand positioning that differentiates you from the next professor in your field.

By leveraging social media effectively, you can establish yourself as an industry leader, build a strong brand identity in the marketplace, and create long-term relationships both online and in person. So, if you're looking to build a successful brand in today's digital age, social media has to be a part of your strategy. To facilitate that, we will cover the implementation of a tried-and-true social media strategy called the 3H system.

An Example: Using Social Media at a High Level

The following is an example of creating and employing your social media strategy at a high level to use your brand assets as the filter through which you post. We will use the brand assets of Dr. Derek Brent, a design and leadership professor, to demonstrate.

Dr. Brent's Brand Assets:

Brand statement: I create experiences for knowledge seekers to feel fearless when they're building something new.

Brand archetype: The Creator

Brand adjectives: Connector, intelligent, social

When thinking about Dr. Brent's overall approach to posting on social media for each piece of content created, he needs to ask himself:

- Is it helping people connect?
- Is it intelligent?
- Is it social?

Each piece of his content does not need to include all three brand adjectives, but it should always include at least one. This signals consistency to his audience, and they then know what to expect when coming to his social media pages. In addition, he'd consider if it is in alignment with his brand promise of "helping people feel fearless when they are building something new." His overall goal would be to bring his ideas and vision to life through his postings, which is in line with the Creator brand archetype.

Therefore, he might write a few paragraphs letting people know about a new app that uses AI to create a 3D model of a living room design based on individual personality types. He then might have a call to action on his post about where people can find and engage with this app.

This type of posting speaks to someone who is a visionary, on top of new design tools in the AI space, and he is connecting his audience to this little-known app.

THE 3H SYSTEM: SOCIAL MEDIA STRATEGY

Google is credited as the originator of the 3H content strategy, having first developed this approach to help YouTube creators produce higher-quality videos for their platform. The system has gained popularity among brand builders and businesses for its effectiveness in fostering a strong online presence. Today, this strategy is embraced by almost every industry and adopted by well-known marketing brands like HubSpot.

The 3H social media strategy helps ensure that

- you use the right platforms to reach the right people;
- you develop a consistent voice across all channels so that when people see something you share, it is "on brand" and recognizable;
- you have information available for viewers to binge when they organically find your postings; and
- what you provide engages your core audience and guides them down a possible sales funnel. (We will take a deep dive into sales funnels in the monetization phase, but for now, just know that a sales funnel is the pathway people take to pay you for something like a speaking engagement, consulting gig, etc.)

This media strategy system consists of three different content categories: help, hero, and hub.

Help Content

Help content aims to build your authority and your audience and generate leads for paid subscribers. At the core of all helping content is its helping nature, thus its name. Each piece follows a problem-solution model that seeks to answer a question or help the audience solve a problem.

This category was originally termed "hygiene content," and has only recently become known as "helping." The term "hygiene" in this context serves as a metaphor for the essential routine practices that contribute to the overall well-being and vitality of a brand's social media presence. Hygiene accurately refers to the publishing frequency for this category, which ranges from three to four times per week or even three to four times per day, if you're being aggressive. Choose a frequency that you can commit to.

Even when easing into such an intense schedule, publishing daily can sound overwhelming. Fortunately, helping content includes a variety of genres and styles, which can help you avoid burnout with any one platform. Examples of helping content often include:

- How-to posts
- Informational carousels
- Infographics

As an academic who helps tenured professors increase their media coverage, I might create a long-form blog post such as *how to find a publisher* or *how to get your book in a brick-and-mortar store*. I can then take that post and break it down into twenty shareable one-sentence tweets on X.

The blog post itself doesn't qualify as social media, but turning the key points of it into an X thread, IG reel, or TikTok video does. I then have a helping blog post and helping social media content that not only answers a question, but also directs users to the long-form content on my website. As you can see, creating help content does not need to be daunting if you use existing assets or repurpose other long-form content.

Hub Content

Whereas help content aims to be discovered organically on search engines like Google or social media platforms like X, hub content seeks to please your existing audience. Like spokes on a wheel, hub content should be consistent. As such, hub content should be posted three to four times a month and can be published on a specific schedule. For example, an economics professor might post his best stock picks every Friday at 5 PM in a five-minute video. He might call this "Stock Pick Friday."

As an additional example of hub content, let's consider an imaginary professor of finance on YouTube. This professor could create a video that gets posted every Monday and shares the top ten finance trends to watch for that week. This professor's audience will come to expect a new video every week and, over time, will not only engage with the content on the YouTube platform but seek out additional content on other platforms. This creates trust as well as credibility and loyalty between the professor and her audience.

There are two primary purposes to remember as you create hub content.

1. **Hub content establishes an ongoing relationship with your audience.** Because this content is published on a regular basis, your audience will come to expect it. This gives them a reason to return to your site and engage over and over. This builds trust and credibility.

2. **Hub content solidifies and expands your brand.** As you create more content, your audience will come to understand more about your brand, the value you offer, your expertise, and more. Over time, this will build brand authority and awareness with your audience.

Remember that it will take more time to create hub content than creating help content. But it doesn't have to be high production like the next category, hero content. Hub content takes longer to create in the 3H social media strategy because it requires consistent, valuable, and engaging information to maintain an online presence and nurture a loyal audience. It involves planning, research, creative effort, and maintaining regular scheduling to ensure ongoing engagement.

Hero Content

Hero content is meant to reach people unfamiliar with your brand—so your first impression must be extraordinary.

If help and hub content are both medium- to high-frequency and low- to medium-production, then hero content is highly produced at a low frequency. Often published three to four times a year or once a quarter, hero content requires a lot of time, effort, and money. This is because this category aims to reach farther than the other two 3H categories, and far beyond your current audience.

Typically, hero content is a video. The high expense associated with this is the result of research, filming, editing, producing, and the other behind-the-scenes tasks required for a well-produced video. This category is often reserved for major product releases or service launches. Ultimately, the potential to drive revenue and awareness and build your audience is what makes such a heavy investment worth it.

As you create your hero content, remember that it will look different for everyone. A financial professor's hero content will look significantly different from a professional snowboarder's.

TIKTOK

The video app TikTok is very popular at the time of writing this book. TikTok can be used for all three types of content if that is your preferred method of engaging with your audience. Here's a brief overview of each component of the strategy that can be implemented on TikTok:

Hero content: Create high-production, attention-grabbing videos that showcase product launches or exciting events. These captivating videos can help generate widespread awareness and engagement on the platform.

Hub content: Regularly publish content that aligns with your brand's niche, connecting with your most loyal followers. For example, if you're a fitness instructor, you could have a weekly series where you share workout routines or healthy recipe ideas. You could even do a short-form cooking tutorial. This content is designed to encourage viewers to come back regularly and establishes you as a reliable source of information.

Help content (hygiene content): Address your audience's needs by providing helpful information such as answering common questions. This will help establish credibility, build trust, and encourage your audience to turn to your TikTok account as a valuable resource.

Three Examples of Hero Content

Apple releases new products annually. Apple consumers expect a major event for the new iPhone every year, on almost the exact same day and week. These events include major changes to the Apple product lineup and software, and the events often take months to produce. The size of both the brand and the event ensures Apple's latest products and innovations are noticed worldwide, in almost every industry, and by consumers far outside of the Apple iPhone market.

Similarly, GoPro is known for its outstanding marketing efforts, particularly with video. Visit GoPro's YouTube channel and you'll find many highly produced videos. While the GoPro product videos feature high-performance athletes, they target a much broader audience and appeal to a lifestyle rather than any single activity. With hero content like theirs, GoPro can inspire, encourage, engage, and appeal to audience members who would otherwise ignore GoPro cameras on a tech aisle shelf.

I use Instagram to talk directly to my creative writers and those who are looking for me to ghostwrite their books. When a new retail store picked up one of my recent books, I hired a videographer and editor to film a commercial for the book placement in the store. I posted the video on my Instagram account to let my audience know about this new opportunity.

Learning About Your Audience After the Implementation of the 3H System

This section shows how you can get to know your followers through the implementation of the 3H system.

By implementing the 3H system consistently, you will be able to get a better understanding of who your followers are and what they want so that you can then funnel them more accurately to your paid services or products and decrease the number of times you need to post daily.

Once you start implementing the 3-H social media system for the busy academic, you'll undoubtedly get more followers and more comments, as well as more people DMing you. People will reach out to you, and when they do, you'll want to get to know them by asking the following types of questions:

- What are your goals?
- What are you working on?
- How far along are you in the process of XYZ?

Imagine how many entrepreneurs or brands actually take the time to ask their followers in a private message what their goals are. Not many.

An Example: Get to Know Your Followers

Here is what this might look like in real life. Bob (fictitious) likes one of my help pieces on Instagram. He messages me saying that he likes the things I am sharing. I reply that there are some additional valuable resources that I think would benefit him. Bob is excited, and within twenty-four hours, I notice that he likes more of my posts on IG. I like a few of his posts in return. My social media strategy already involves giving free educational advice around the topic of writing, as I am clear on my brand and my brand strategy on that platform. So while he is looking at my IG posts, he's getting even more value.

After a few days, I see that Bob leaves another message under one of my posts. I follow up by sending him another direct message about the comment he left. I take the time to ask him questions like: "What are you working on, Bob?" and "I see you liked my comic book writing reel. I'd love to assist you in your writing journey. Where are you in the process with your comic book?" Bob tells me a little more about what he is working on.

From here, I have a few options. If I can further help Bob, I send him a link to my paid coaching and strategy call sessions, or I direct him to a course I have, if it is directly related to something he has mentioned. However, **the most beneficial thing I have learned from Bob is what he is looking for.** Bob might respond to my questions like this: "I'm trying to convert my novel into a graphic novel. That's why I liked the advice you shared," or "Your content is great, but I'm having trouble with clearly identifying the motives behind the villain in my story." This information is a gold mine for me. I can now create a social post answering his question directly, or I can create a course around this topic if I have gotten this feedback from multiple people. I can do a range of other things with this information.

I've learned what one person in my audience needs so that I can add more value to his life as well as others'. If one person is facing this challenge, you investigate if others are as well by using this same engagement strategy. There are so many ways you can implement feedback from people like Bob into your sales funnel and overall social media strategy.

By the way, Bob is now what you would consider a "true fan," which we will learn more about in Chapter 8: "1,000 True Fans."

Document Your Data to Cater Your Content

After each interaction with people like Bob, you want to document what you've learned in a spreadsheet by keeping track of the questions and problems they are having. That way, going forward, you can start to see patterns that will help you with product and service development. If different people are asking you the same types of questions, you know it is valuable to cover that material for your audience. The key is to interact with your fans and document, document, document.

The other way that you could better understand your community through the implementation of this social media strategy is by using data from Facebook. Facebook captures a lot of data, and one of the things that I teach in the Power Your Research program is that when you have a high-level blog or op-ed published in an online news outlet, it's a good idea to use the boost post function on Facebook or create a simple Facebook ad to get that article in front of more people. Or, if you were featured in a high-level international press outlet such as *Good Morning America*, or even a niche blog that has millions of followers, you'll want to boost posts or run ads on Facebook to get more people to engage with that article. You're not selling anything, but what you're doing is building brand awareness to get more eyes on your article.

And the great thing about Facebook is that ads allow you to target different people who are specifically interested in your topic. When you run these Facebook ads, you're going to get data, and this data is going give you a breakdown of gender, age, and likes, saves, shares, etc. These demographic breakdowns and engagement metrics can give you insights into the type of people clicking on your links and sharing your content, which you can then use to better understand your target audience.

If I see that 70 percent of women engaged with my article and only 30 percent of men, I know that women in a specific age range are my audience, at least for the topic that the article is about. This is a valuable data point that you then can use when creating social media content and implementing digital media strategy.

You can take this demographic information and start to create content around the psychographics of this particular audience—women in a certain age range. For example, women in academe have a different set of issues than men in academe. That means it's okay in my messaging for me to talk about the discrepancies in what men get paid for speaking engagements versus women, if I know women are my primary audience. In this way, you can better tailor the material you post. When we get to the monetization phase of this book (Chapter 9), we will revisit social media, specifically looking at how to turn your followers into clients and customers through an Instagram sales funnel.

THE DIFFUSION OF INNOVATION THEORY

In this chapter, you've learned why socials matter in your brand-building process, how to implement an effective social media strategy, and how to get to know your audience while implementing the 3H strategy. These three components are critical to connecting with your audience. However, there is one other critical framework that I find important to help you understand the long tail of any social media strategy.

Doing the hard work of posting consistently on social media can be exhausting and daunting at times. As you can see, you are learning about your audience by putting out content until you know more precisely what your audience wants and needs. During this implementation and learning phase, it can be tempting to want to focus more on generating followers instead of targeting your current followers. **It is important that you focus on what really matters, which is giving the most value to the people who are early adopters of your content.**

Ironically, focusing on your early followers is what will propel you to reaching a critical mass of people. As such, the Diffusion of Innovation theory is ideal to cover at this juncture so you remain clear on how to get your brand messaging to spread. The Diffusion of Innovation theory is a framework that teaches us the importance of connecting to our current fans and followers, and it makes a great case for doing so.

What Is the Diffusion of Innovation Theory?

This theory is the study of how, why, and at what rate new ideas and technology spread. The theory is based on the idea that innovations are adopted by different groups at different rates depending on their psychographics and personalities, among other factors, and it was first introduced by Everett Rogers in 1962. It remains an incredibly useful tool for marketers to understand how to promote their products or services.

The theory has three main elements: innovation, communication channels, and social systems. The Diffusion of Innovation theory can be applied to any industry or product that needs to be marketed, including your academic brand.

The first element is the idea or invention itself (your brand). The second element is the communication channels that are used to share information about the innovation (social media). And the third element is the social system in which people live and work (a targeted population or group of people). When opening any marketing or communication book, the model will look like this:

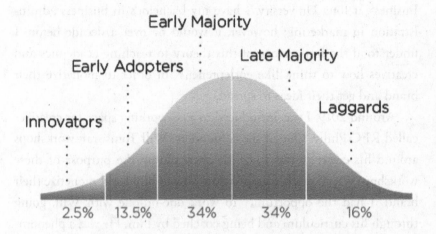

Early Majority

Late Majority

Early Adopters

Laggards

Innovators

2.5%   13.5%   34%   34%   16%

INNOVATION ADOPTION LIFECYCLE

You might be thinking: What does this have to do with social media strategy? I am glad you asked. Every time I revisit this framework, I am reminded that I always need to focus on the people who are currently my fans and my audience. So often, we can get so focused on reaching the masses (the middle of the diagram) that we forget that we have some loyal fans and supporters right now.

I had been used to thinking about the Diffusion of Innovation theory in terms of big brands and big products, but it's actually very useful in thinking about your own personal academic brand and how you can grow it. And more importantly, the things that you should be focusing on in order to grow your brand at scale.

My Story

As a professor of communication, I have long taught the Diffusion of Innovation theory in courses such as Communication Theory and Health Communication. I learned about Diffusion of Innovation theory as an undergraduate studying marketing at the LaPenta School of

Business at Iona University. I have my bachelor's in business admin-istration in marketing; however, it would be over a decade before I understood the importance of this theory to teaching academics and creatives how to think like entrepreneurs in order to monetize their brand and get their ideas to spread.

Around 2019, I was introduced to a co-working space for creatives called REC Philly. One of the cofounders, Will Toms, ran workshops around his creative strategy guide curriculum. The purpose of these workshops was to teach entrepreneurs how to build and monetize their brand. I had the opportunity to work one-on-one with Will, going through his curriculum and being coached by him. He was a phenom-enal creative coach who largely inspired this book as well as what has come to be known as Power Your Research. It was through learning his curriculum that the Diffusion of Innovation theory was reintroduced to me as **a way to understand how to grow my following and get my brand in front of a larger audience**.

Will was able to show me how to actually apply this theory to my social media strategy, as well as my larger goals. It changed the game for me by showing me what is truly important when it comes to social media.

The Stages of Diffusion of Innovation Theory

Looking more in depth at the characteristics of each group of people across the Diffusion of Innovation model is helpful in clarifying how to build off the current fans you have or the innovators who will be the first to discover and support you.

Innovators

The theory states that innovators are the first to adopt new things (tech-nologies, ideas, music, etc.), but there are many different reasons why this might be the case.

Some innovators have a natural curiosity and love for new things, while others may see potential financial gain in being an early adopter, or they may get access to new technologies through work, hobbies, or personal connections. **Innovators are your first followers on socials.** In fact, innovators are the first 2.5 percent of a group to adopt a new idea.

Innovators are usually open-minded and willing to try out new things. They also have a higher social status (not in economic terms but in influence in your niche area) than other people in your niche area, which means they can influence others to adopt the product or idea as well. So you want to make sure that the people who are your innovators love what you offer so much that you become a celebrity to them. You serve them well. You make them happy. When they are happy, what happens next is magic.

Innovators convince early adopters to try your thing, to follow you. Imagine your innovators saying to someone at work or at a party, "You don't know Dr. Jane Doe? You HAVE to follow her on LinkedIn," or "You don't know Dr. Howard? Her book changed my life as a professor. You HAVE to get it."

The best form of flattery is someone recommending to their friends that they engage with your brand or try your service. So, while many brands are focused on reaching the middle of the bell curve and getting more and more followers so that the majority will accept and like their idea, cause, or brand, they are actually focused on the wrong thing. You can't reach the masses unless you can get the innovators first.

Early Adopters

The next 13.5 percent to adopt an innovation are the early adopters. This small group is important because these people are the ones who will allow your idea or brand to grow beyond a small percentage of the population.

These people are usually opinion leaders in their communities, and they have a high status as well. (Again, not in economic terms, but in influence and persuasion.) They often try out new products because they want to be seen as trendsetters among their peers. However, they learn about these new ideas, brands, and services from the innovators. The innovators already tried it out, gave feedback, and suggested it to the early adopters.

Now your brand, product, or service is growing because this segment makes up more of the ecosystem you are operating in. You do a great job with serving (help content) and inspiring this larger group; now you can move through the model to reach the early majority next.

Early Majority

This group is made up of people who don't want to be left behind by the latest trends, but they don't want to be seen as followers either. This psychological understanding of this group is a key factor when trying to grow your brand.

Being consistent and having longevity means something to people. It communicates that you are the real deal. That you are trustworthy, reliable, and credible (hub content). Without a long-term presence in the marketplace, people will not adopt the product or service, which means that it will be difficult to grow in popularity and find success. This is where **social proof** comes into play.

Social Proof

Social proof refers to a psychological and social phenomenon where people copy the actions of others when trying to make the "right" choice in a given situation. For example, if you are trying to hire a plumber, noticing that they have over four hundred reviews on Google and most of them are five stars will probably make you more likely to hire them. Why? It demonstrates that lots of other people have previously made the same choice and come out on top for it, and it reassures you that you aren't making a mistake by choosing them as well.

Do you have testimonials from the innovators, early adopters, and early majority? Are they commenting on your posts? Do you have a track record of showing up with a consistent message? Is your social media consistent? Have you been putting out that blog over and over again for years? Proving that you will be there and show up is what people are looking for if they are going to invest time and money into you and your thing.

Late Majority

This is the group of people who adopt an innovation after the early adopters and the early majority. The late majority is usually more cautious about adopting new innovations than the previous groups. They may be slower to adopt because they don't want to be seen as foolish or uninformed, or because they are not convinced that the innovation will work for them.

This is the group of people who might come to a Power Your Research call after being referred or seeing it work online and asking the questions, "How do you know this would work for me?" or "How long have you been doing this work?" or "I need to talk to a colleague to see what they think."

These are the people who will leave similar comments on your help content. This group cares a lot about other people's opinions and perceptions when they are deciding to make a purchase or become a believer. Fitting in is an important element in human psychology, despite people seeking to stand out. What many actually want is to be accepted. To be seen as smart. To be seen as right.

The late majority is typically more conservative in their views than early adopters or innovators. They are skeptical of change and often resist adopting new technologies or ideas because they fear being left behind or missing out on something better.

A great example of this is a tweet I was mentioned in recently. It had gone viral, and some women had a visceral reaction to the fact that

I teach women with advanced degrees to charge at least $3,500 for a one-hour talk. Women were advocating to devalue themselves, even going as far as saying they wouldn't talk to other women in academia who actually charged for their labor and time when doing speaking engagements. That thinking is an example of the late majority for me because those people want to fit in. They want to stay in their place. They are using a belief as a fact because this new information challenges the core of their limiting beliefs around what society (and academia) tells them about who they are and what their value is.

The late majority will be more likely to buy a product if it has been endorsed by a trusted person, if it is cheaper than other products, or if they have seen it used by someone they know. The late majority is typically more risk averse than innovators, but they also have a greater need for the innovation. People view following you on socials the same way. They value their attention, time, and who they follow. It is a personal choice that they believe reflects who they are and what they desire to see on our social media feeds.

If your content or your community doesn't reflect these values or needs, then they won't follow you. The late majority is often skeptical of new ideas and products, but they will eventually adopt them if they see enough evidence that something will be beneficial to them. This group is more likely to buy from a company that has been around for a while and has a good reputation.

Laggards

The laggards are the people who are the last to adopt a new innovation. They are not necessarily resistant to change, but they have a slower rate of adoption. In order to convince the laggards, you need to understand their needs and how they differ from those of innovators and early adopters. You also need to understand what motivates them and what they want out of life.

Laggards often lack interest in new things. They may be skeptical about innovations because they don't want change or they don't see any benefits in them.

In order to convince the laggards, it's important for you to understand their needs and find ways of meeting them without changing their habits too much.

The Takeaway

What's best to take away from this model is that you need to focus on your current client, customer, follower, and fan. **Do not chase the majority before you can overdeliver to your innovators and early adopters.** Those are the groups of people who will throw you over to the masses, as long as you stay consistent, reliable, and dedicated to them.

The Diffusion of Innovation theory is typically used by big businesses to move products through this cycle, but I have found it especially relevant to social media strategy. Whether it is monetizing a coaching business, consulting business, or beyond, you need to understand the psychology behind each group in this model so you can move your product, service, and/or brand through the phases to make impact at scale.

As you've learned in this chapter, building your brand in the social media environment is about that psychological connection to your existing audience. Now you are ready to move on to landing media coverage. This is an important next step because media coverage will allow more people to discover you and your work outside of just posting on social media. You will now be in a position to engage people effectively as you appear in the media, and as they seek you out on social media. In addition, your media appearances will be in alignment with what they find when they reach your social media accounts because of the clarity and structure you have now created.

CHAPTER 6

Media Coverage

F or me, media coverage refers to the amount of attention given by various forms of media, such as news outlets, television programs, radio shows, online news portals, and podcasts. Media coverage can be measured in terms of how much coverage or exposure a particular person, event, or issue is receiving from the media. **While some consider social media as media coverage, in this book, I do not.** Media coverage involves traditional or digital outlets, where journalists, producers, and reporters cover stories about brands, products, and/or events. While social media offers more control and direct engagement, media coverage brings external validation and reaches wider audiences through established news and other media channels. Both channels are valuable and can complement each other in building a brand and gaining visibility.

At this stage:

- You understand who you are as a brand.
- You have the building blocks to engage on social media with the people who matter the most.

- You have a clear idea of the messaging that works for your audience.
- You know your overall life vision or the reason you are doing this work in the first place.
- You are clear on your mission, vision, and purpose.

Now it is time to **step up your game and start disseminating your messaging across various media outlets.**

The great news is that once people hear or see you in the media, they will be *delighted* that you already have active social media pages they can explore to get more of what they heard you talk about in the media interview, op-ed, etc. This is why it is so important to address these building blocks early on, **before** throwing yourself out there. Imagine someone hearing me talk about academic branding on a radio interview, only to go to my LinkedIn profile and see ten images of my bird-watching hobby. That would immediately confuse them, and I will have lost a potential follower, fan, and/or customer.

The breadth of the media coverage you receive matters. Media coverage brings more people into your network, and it allows more people to know you exist so they can further engage with you and your work. This chapter covers:

- Why media coverage is important for academics
- How media coverage helps increase your visibility
- Two strategic frameworks for understanding how to get high-level media coverage
- How to pitch podcasts

WHY MEDIA COVERAGE IS IMPORTANT FOR ACADEMICS

For academics, getting featured in the media for your work increases research citations. Yet many academics simply do not appreciate the value of media coverage and find it a distraction from the "real" work of doing research, teaching classes, and presenting at academic conferences.

BlueSky public relations firm notes, "Not every member of faculty will share your passion for media relations or press coverage. In fact, many will not see the benefit at all. With their own research projects and teaching demands eating up their time, a request to write an op-ed or have an interview can be yet another thing to add to a lengthy to-do list."[18]

However, media coverage is not a distraction! It is actually an asset for you in this fast-paced, ever-changing higher-ed landscape. Professors who get media coverage for their articles, research in general, books, and more actually see an increase in the number of times they are cited by other academics.

An analysis of over eight hundred academic research papers on physical health and exercise suggests that the level of popular media coverage for a given paper is strongly linked to the attention it receives within the scientific community.[19]

In my own work, my book *Black Comics: Politics of Race and Representation* has been cited the most, and it is also the book that has been featured in the media most frequently.

Your academic friends are consumers of media just like everyone else, and when our work appears in places like the *New York Times*, the *Washington Post*, and even small, niche podcasts, it hits the ears of your colleagues. This, in turn, alerts them to your research.

In addition to media coverage being important to your research articles and books within academia, it is also important to bring more people into your network so that you can increase your credibility and, ultimately, income.

In short, the more mechanisms you can use to get your name and work in front of people around the world, the more you put yourself in a position to enjoy new opportunities. If people do not know about you, they cannot work with you.

Getting media coverage is a passion of mine, and I find great joy in being able to "crack the code," so to speak. That is, pitching an outlet on why I am the perfect person to appear on their show, and then getting the invite, is a thrill for me. I know that might not be the case for everyone. You might feel like pitching is a thankless job, and that's okay. As long as you feel the work is important enough to get the result you desire, you will stay the course and find the motivation to put a strategy in place to get consistent media coverage.

HOW MEDIA COVERAGE HELPS INCREASE YOUR VISIBILITY

Let's next look at how media placements help in terms of building your brand. Doing the work to get this media coverage requires a lot of time and effort. However, if I can make clear how individual media placements accumulate to have a big impact on your brand's visibility, it will most likely keep you motivated to do the work involved in pitching yourself.

This section can be summed up in one formula:

media coverage = compounding interest

Media coverage is to your brand what compounding interest is to your finances. Let's break it down.

When you invest $1,000 into a savings account that has a 5 percent compounding interest rate, at the end of year one, you will have $1,050. And then, at the end of year two, you will get 5 percent on the initial deposit plus the $50 gain. Now, I know in this analogy no one has a 5 percent compounding interest rate on their savings account these days, but the point remains. That initial investment grows and works for you each year that money sits in your account. That initial investment is working for you long term.

Well, that's the same way media coverage works. Once you learn the strategies to landing media spots, you will benefit from the compounding interest effect over and over again, because today **your media placements live online for the entirety of your life and beyond.** This allows your hard work in getting the initial media placement to keep working for you until you eventually get to a point where you no longer have to consistently execute media placement strategies in the future.

Eventually, you will no longer need to pitch yourself to large platforms like NBC, BBC, and ABC because when they are looking for someone to speak in the area of your expertise, your brand is already strong enough that they will find you as soon as they go searching. Or even better, they will search for you by name. You can then spend your time on other important areas of your brand—like increasing your income.

My Story

ABC news in the city of Philadelphia, where I live, once did a short news story on a comic book I had written. ABC news is obviously a high-level media placement—it has name recognition both nationally and internationally. What most people don't know is that it is someone's job in media and news companies to look through local news affiliates' media coverage to find interesting stories.

So, a news reporter was spending her nights poring through local news coverage and found my local ABC news story. The reporter then reached out to me to do a similar story on *Good Morning America* digital, a media platform with national and international coverage. Once that article dropped, I benefited from the compounding interest effect, which generated an even bigger media spot that allowed me to reach thousands more. I likely reached millions more people without having to do any additional pitching or work, not to mention all of the affiliates that picked up the initial story along the way.

Early on, larger platforms will most likely always require you to pitch. However, as you do the work, this will change. Power Your Research clients who have worked tirelessly to follow the media placement strategies and concepts in this chapter get to a place where they do not need to regularly pitch media outlets anymore. Thus, they have the time to dedicate to sales-generating activities, writing books, and more of the things they love to do.

If, however, they want to be on larger shows more consistently, they will reengage in pitching themselves using the strategies here, with more attention to high-level placements.

In addition, if I want to be on a particular podcast or media outlet, I will certainly pitch myself. Sometimes, I put high-level media outlets on my vision board. My strategy today is more targeted and focused on the international and nationally recognized media of my choice. Popular podcasts, not necessarily in my area of expertise, are also of high interest to me.

If you land enough media spots in the niche area that you want to be known for, you will enjoy the fruits of your labor in this same way; that is, coverage across hundreds if not thousands of media outlets with one simple investment of your time. The quicker you get started on this, the quicker you will enjoy the results.

TWO STRATEGIC FRAMEWORKS FOR GETTING HIGH-LEVEL MEDIA COVERAGE

There are two strategic frameworks to help you understand how you can access the highest level of media coverage. The first concept is what I call "the Ladder Effect," and the second is how status roles play into media placements.

The reason I teach the underlying concepts behind getting media coverage before delving into actual tactics is that the concepts will enable you to actually shape a customized strategy. You need a vision (which you have), a strategy for accessing media, and then you need the tactics (actions) to get you there.

Learning the tactics is not useful if you do not have a strategy in place first that is connected to your vision. As I go over the Ladder Effect and status roles, I advise you to jot down notes and ideas in terms of a game plan for employing these strategies on your own.

The Ladder Effect

The Ladder Effect will assist you in developing a game plan to get media coverage. It will lend itself to the ultimate strategy that you employ to land the placements that are important to you and your brand.

I teach my clients to think about what a ladder is for. It is designed to step up, one rung at a time, in order to reach a specific destination. Each rung brings you closer to reaching the destination you want. However, you can't skip rungs. The only way to get to the top of the ladder is to take it one by one. If you try to skip some, you may fall or otherwise have a negative result that will not allow you to reach your destination. This is the way you need to think about getting media coverage.

You want to start on the first rung and work your way up. In this metaphor, **the first rungs of the ladder are local media outlets.** Why? Because it is easier for you to access them, and they can provide huge returns on your sweat equity.

Local newspapers, TV shows, and podcasts are typically eager to have local experts talk about their work. In fact, they are constantly seeking people in the community willing to come on and speak with their audience. They simply do not yet know you exist and do not know you are interested.

Your goal on this first rung is to reach out to as many hosts, producers, and journalists in your local community (think neighborhood newspapers too) to ask if you can write an op-ed for their paper or blog or appear in an interview. (Don't forget about your local NPR affiliate, which many academics see as an important outlet for their brand.)

You might consider this fruitless because you may think smaller outlets do not have much reach. However, they do.

A Few Examples: The Ladder Effect

One of my clients, Dr. Rachel Bowen, a professor who focuses on gender equity, compiled a list of smaller media outlets that she could write op-eds for. My client included the *Seattle Times* on her list, wrote an op-ed, and pitched it. She was successful, and as a result, her opinion piece "Why Do Working Moms Earn Less and Do More?" was published in the *Seattle Times*, receiving over fifty comments in the online discussion section.

Because of technology, we are not limited solely to printed newspapers, where only the people who pick up a physical copy get access to our work. In this way, even smaller outlets, such as the *Seattle Times*, can have massive reach online, catapulting your career and visibility.

Using this strategy consistently, Dr. Bowen can use these types of local media placements to pitch larger newspapers like the *New York Times*. These smaller outlets, along with consistent placements, help establish credibility.

In addition, producers running podcasts in your local town or city may have small audiences today; however, in a year, they may have gained a huge audience. If so, your interview will enjoy the success of the podcast's growth because it was already in the pipeline, and new users can find it if they're browsing previous podcasts.

These smaller outlets will give you the credibility to move up to the next rung. For example, if you appear on a podcast that has one thousand downloads a month, you can now pitch yourself to a podcast that has a slightly larger audience and use that previous interview as evidence that you are a great guest. Thus, you're moving up the ladder little by little until you are appearing on podcasts, radio shows, and so on that have significantly larger reaches.

I spent years doing podcast and radio interviews on shows that had very small audiences; however, it is the collection of those small outlets around my specific area of interest that allowed me to build great discoverability on Google because the sheer number of those smaller outlets added up to a significant cluster around a specific topic.

And while we will talk about landing a TEDx talk in the next chapter—including explaining the difference between a TED Talk and a TEDx talk—it's worth mentioning how starting out local can lead to significant traction. Brené Brown, world-renowned research professor, went viral for her first TEDx talk in 2010. Brown is from Texas. Her first TEDx talk, *The Power of Vulnerability*, was presented in Houston. I can guarantee you that Brown, unknown at the time, had a significantly higher chance of landing a local (in Houston) opportunity, as opposed to landing a TEDx opportunity in New York or any other place in the country.

Similarly for me, while my TEDx talk is not one of the top five most viewed, like Brown's, as of the writing of this book, it has more than thirteen thousand views on the Ted.com website and YouTube.

When I decided to pitch myself for a TEDx talk, I knew focusing on an event in Philadelphia, where I am from, would give me a better chance of success, rather than pitching myself to a conference in another part of the country.

Even if you have had a sprinkle of media placements on BBC, ABC, and other recognizable outlets, you still need to start local because those larger outlets are not yet consistent for you. The way you get consistent invitations to national and international outlets is to carve out discoverability in the online sphere, where your brand is attached to the keywords you want to be known for, so that when journalists and producers type those keywords into Google, your name comes up. You do this by starting small, using each step of the ladder as leverage until you are at the top of the ladder.

Status Roles

Now that you understand the underlying strategic framework on how to go about getting media coverage, this section explains some of the psychology behind pitching yourself as you climb the ladder.

Status roles refer to the positions individuals occupy in society or within a particular organization or group, which are often associated with varying levels of power, influence, and prestige. Status roles can be formal, such as job titles or official positions within an organization, or informal, such as being recognized as a leader or influencer within a particular community.

The status that comes with a particular role can be conferred by various factors, such as education, wealth, reputation, or social connections. Those who occupy higher status roles often have greater access to resources, opportunities, and decision-making power than those who occupy perceived lower-status roles.

Status roles can have a significant impact on an individual's success, as those in high-status roles may be more likely to receive recognition, respect, and opportunities, while those in perceived lower-status roles may face barriers and limitations.

While I had been instinctively using status roles to climb the ladder of media coverage, I didn't have a name for it, and I didn't think about it critically. I was just doing it naturally. I first began to pay attention to status roles after listening to Seth Godin discuss the concept on his podcast *Akimbo*. Godin has written extensively about the importance of status roles in achieving success.

He says, "Status roles are at the core of who we are. They change how we spend our time, our money and most of all, our imaginations.

We define ourselves in relative terms, not absolute ones. More stuff, more power, less this or less that."[20]

And this is all great news for you because in this metaphor (if you will), each media placement is a form of status. And once you have a cluster of media placements around a subject area in combination with your advanced degree, you gain even more benefits of your status in your area.

In essence, Godin is saying that people who hold perceived status often have advantages that help them achieve success more easily than those who don't. These advantages can include things like access to opportunities, greater freedom to take risks, and more decision-making power. Once someone has achieved status, they may be more likely to continue achieving success because they have developed the tools and perception necessary to do so.

My Story

In 2016, I was interviewed on *The Breakfast Club*, a radio talk show hosted by Charlamagne tha God, Angela Yee (previously), and DJ Envy. The show airs on the nationally syndicated radio network iHeartRadio's Power 105.1 FM in New York City. The show, which debuted in 2010, features interviews with celebrities, musicians, and influencers, as well as discussions on current events, pop culture, and lifestyle topics. Its popularity has continued to grow since its launch, and it is now one of the most popular morning shows in the country.

This was a big interview for me—maybe my biggest at the time—but previous to this appearance, I had already been featured in the *Washington Post*, the *LA Times,* and other high-end outlets. I had also climbed the ladder by doing tons of small podcasts and radio shows (with some of these smaller shows blowing up in popularity afterwards). So, by the time I started pitching *The Breakfast Club*, I had a number of media placements that conferred status was equivalent to what the show's producers would consider acceptable. I would have had very low odds of landing that media opportunity if I did not have a history of high-level media outlets. It was the status that my previous appearances conveyed that significantly increased the odds.

In essence, my brand said, "People like me belong on shows like this." That very statement is about perceived status. Therefore, the name of the game is about using that perceived status to your advantage and leveraging it to climb the ladder.

While we will cover tactics on how to pitch yourself, it's imperative to understand that you convey your "status" in your pitches to media. In short, this is no time to be humble. It's time to leverage your status.

HOW TO PITCH PODCASTS

You might be wondering why I am focusing heavily on podcasts here. First, while I'd love to, this book cannot cover the steps for landing each type of media placement (op-eds, TV interviews, etc.); however, once you learn the strategic concepts of how to think about pitching, the tactics here are transferrable to any type of media coverage you seek. Second, podcasts are going to be one of the first rungs of the ladder, and they're the perfect place to start.

Podcasts have seen significant growth in popularity in recent years and have become a very accessible form of entertainment and education. In fact, many of my favorite ways to listen to NPR shows are the replays on their podcasts. While radio still remains a popular medium, particularly for local news, sports, and music, podcasts have gained ground due to their on-demand nature and the ability to access a wide variety of topics from all over the world.

According to a 2021 report by Edison Research, approximately eighty million Americans—28 percent of the US population ages twelve and above—are now weekly podcast listeners, a 17 percent increase over 2020. The overall monthly podcast listening audience is now more diverse than ever: 57 percent of monthly podcast listeners are white, 16 percent Latino, 13 percent African American, 4 percent Asian, and 10 percent of some other background. Sixty-two percent of the US population ages twelve and older, around 176 million people, are now weekly online audio listeners, an all-time high for this category.[21] These numbers continue to grow; as of 2023, new research from Edison has found that 31 percent of Americans ages twelve and above have listened to a podcast in the last week, up from 28 percent in 2022. It is more than likely that this trend will increase over the coming years.

The odds that you can use a number of your podcast interviews as leverage to climb the ladder are extremely high, and you can also control the types of podcasts you target, focusing only on active and well-known podcasts as a part of your strategy.

The last reason I am focusing on podcasts is that a podcast can go viral at any time, and you will benefit from podcasters who are consistently building their brands and are in it for the long haul.

SEO

It's worth noting that some small podcasts can have great SEO—search engine optimization. SEO is the process of affecting the visibility of a website or a web page in a search engine's unpaid results—often referred to as "natural," "organic," or "earned" results. The higher a site is ranked on search engines, the more visitors to that particular site, and this will lead to more people finding you. You need to think of media coverage, including smaller outlets, as a way to build your niche and actually create SEO. SEO is important because when someone searches your topic area of expertise via Google, you want something about you to come up on the first or second page. That is the goal. The small shows are great preparation for the bigger platforms. Doing a lot of interviews with smaller podcasts around the internet increases the links to your website and other content. This will allow the algorithm on search engines to connect you with your area of expertise. In 2023, I received an "Introduction to Google SEO" certificate from the University of California, Davis, through the online learning platform Coursera. I highly recommend a course like this if you'd like to learn more about SEO and brand building.

THE POWER YOUR RESEARCH FOUR-STEP SYSTEM TO SUCCESSFULLY PITCH PODCASTS

Now that you understand the strategy, it's time to implement my four-step system to landing podcast interviews. As you work though this section, take note of how you can transfer this framework to other types of media coverage that you want to include as a part of your media placement strategy.

1. Know Your Brand and Key Terms

Since you have been following the Power Your Research process, you already know this information, but it's worth a refresher here, as identifying specific podcasts in your area is crucial to your success. Get clear on who your target audience is and what you want to convey to them. For example, since my academic work is in representation in comics, I am clear that I need to find podcasts that focus on the comic book audience and those that also view representation as important. Additionally, using a clear example such as Brené Brown, the key terms for her brand are "vulnerability" and "dealing with shame." Therefore, she'd be targeting podcasts that discuss these specific areas.

2. Create Your Podcast List

Once you have a good understanding of who you are trying to reach and what you want to be talking about, you need to develop a list of podcasts in your niche and secure the email addresses to pitch these podcasts. I believe in outsourcing these types of tasks, as this is not the best use of our time. If you want to outsource this, you have two options. You can hire an assistant to research and create a list of forty to one hundred podcasts, or you can use a freelance site like Fiverr.com to hire someone to do this for you (the option I teach my clients). There are numerous contractors on Fiverr.com that do this specific work at a reasonable rate.

3. Reach Out to the Host

Now that you have the contact details and your list, you need to reach out to these podcasts. When making contact, you need to be clear and concise in your email. What you are communicating to the host is

- that you're a fan of their show or you like what they are doing,
- why their audience needs to hear from you, and
- your credentials (status).

Here is a sample email that you can feel free to use. I sent this to podcasters when I was promoting my book *Nina's Whisper* (a novel about same-sex domestic abuse). The email is broken down into parts to help you understand the intent of each section.

Part One: State why you like their show

> Dear [Name],
>
> I hope you are well. I came across your podcast recently and really like what you've put together. So, on behalf of your audience, thank you! I listened to a few of your episodes, and I appreciate how you offer your audience something new and different—it's valuable.

Part Two: State why you are contacting them and how your pitch relates to their audience

I'm writing to you because I would love to be a guest on your show.

Recently, I published a novel, *Nina's Whisper*, that untangles the psychology of abuse; however, the book is rare and unique because it is about same-sex domestic abuse. Even though female-to-female abuse is largely ignored, the Human Rights Campaign estimates that 44 percent of lesbians experience domestic abuse. In addition, the CDC estimates that domestic abuse in LGBTQ relationships has higher rates than that of heterosexual couples. I believe your audience will appreciate this conversation because the focus of your podcast is all about female empowerment and self-care.

Part Three: State your credentials/status

Through my platform, I aim to challenge our notion of who can be a victim and challenge the script that abuse is only male to female. I have a large social media presence of over 4.5K followers on X, including millions of impressions monthly between my Instagram, Facebook, and X accounts. I have also been featured on/in major media outlets, such as, but not limited to, BBC World, ABC, PBS, NPR, NBC, the *Los Angeles Times*, the *Washington Post*, *The Breakfast Club,* and more.

I would love to share my own personal story as well as the significance of my book, *Nina's Whisper,* with your listeners. I hope to not only bring awareness to your listeners but also inspire them to triumph over the trauma of abuse.

> To learn more about me, I invite you to view my website here: www.sheenachoward.com and my electronic press kit HERE.
>
> I look forward to your reply and a chance to be a guest on your show.
>
> Warmest regards,

You can handle getting these emails out by sending them yourself (which is what I have historically done). This will likely take a couple of hours each week if you want to send one hundred emails. You can bring on an intern or pay an assistant to send these out for you if you do not want to invest time in this endeavor. The last step of this process is critical, and that is to follow up.

4. Follow up

If you don't hear back from the host after a few days, follow up with a polite and friendly message. It's important to stay persistent but avoid being pushy. Remember, success is in the follow-up. People are busy. Sometimes emails inadvertently go to spam folders when they are from strangers, or people can simply forget to respond to you. Never assume that the person doesn't want you as a guest. You need to follow up over a few days until you get a yes or a no.

After making contact with each of these podcast outlets, you will undoubtedly get opportunities to be interviewed. Your job now is to make sure you are cooperative and available for scheduling these appearances. Today, many podcast interviews can be done virtually. I highly recommend, though, that for local podcasts, you try to make it in person to the studio, as this will allow you to film your interview and use it as social media content later. No matter what you decide, do your best to secure the interview when you get a favorable response.

TO GET PAID OR NOT TO GET PAID

I once heard an academic advise other academics that they shouldn't do podcasts if they aren't getting paid to do the interview. This couldn't be further from the truth.

A podcast interview is an equal exchange. You are getting in front of someone else's audience to grow your fan base, and in return, the podcaster is creating an engaging interview and getting to talk to you to grow their audience.

If you do not think appearing on a specific podcast is worth your time, then don't do the interview, but getting paid to do a podcast interview is extremely rare.

Media coverage is essential for academics to communicate their research to a broader audience, to secure funding, and to enhance their reputations. By sharing your work with the public, you can contribute to important debates and have a greater impact on society.

CHAPTER 7

Visibility

To build a strong brand, it is essential to have a comprehensive strategy that focuses on increasing visibility across platforms that matter to you and your audience. This increases your chances of success. High visibility is crucial for academics who wish to make an impact beyond their academic circles. By accessing platforms that are ubiquitous to your target audience and/or important to society at large, academics have the opportunity to share their research and ideas with a wider audience.

Media coverage is only one way to increase your visibility. Therefore, here we will talk about securing access to platforms that will strengthen the credibility and authority of your brand. I'll also put a spotlight on two other platforms that will help elevate your brand: landing a TEDx talk and getting physical books on bookstore shelves.

Why TEDx and bookstores?

First, if you are reading this book, you are my target audience—academics or those with PhDs. As such, over the years, you have shown me that you value the TED Talk platform. It is a platform that many aspire to access, and even if you do not want to do a TEDx or TED Talk, you at least value the platform as a place to establish credibility.

Second, getting books into brick-and-mortar stores is an area I am focusing on because many PhDs either have books published or know they will publish one in the future. It's basically what we do!

Even if you are not interested in either of these two platforms, this chapter will still be valuable, as you will use the techniques learned here to apply to the platforms you deem of more value to your specific audience.

WHAT IS VISIBILITY?

I'm using the word "visibility" here to refer to platforms that are credible to your specific audience. To build authority, you need to access places and spaces that make you an authority figure with your audience. For example, when I appeared on *The Breakfast Club*, that platform gave me significant authority and credibility with a specific demographic and audience. However, lots of people reading this book may have never even heard of that show, and that's okay because I went on that podcast for credibility with a different audience. Therefore, I want you to think about visibility in terms of the places you and your work can appear that make you a superstar in the eyes of your target audience.

I want to take some more time here to explore why visibility is important to building your brand.

Visibility Can Help Differentiate You from Your Peers

When a brand is visible, it stands out from the crowd and creates a unique identity. For instance, a brand that uses a specific color or logo consistently across all its marketing channels can create a recognizable identity that sets it apart from its competitors.

By doing so, it can make it easier for customers to identify and remember the brand. While I do not cover logo design and website colors here, at this stage in the Power Your Research process, it is important to consider these things. You already have a clear idea of who you are, what you stand for, and who you serve. In addition, you now know how to land media placements. Therefore, the consistency of your logo design will become something that people can easily remember when they see it on your platforms.

Your physical presence matters, too, in terms of recognition and consumer recall. We all remember Steve Jobs's "uniform"; it was a part of his brand. No matter what platform he appeared on, you can probably still visualize his black shirt and blue jeans.

As you focus on combining media coverage and visibility, create something physical that allows you to stand out. For me, I wear colorful and memorable earrings. When people see me, they say, "You always have the best earrings." That is what I have decided on as my physical representation of my brand; in addition to my brand colors of red, black, and white, and my logo.

MAXIMIZE VISIBILITY

There are certain platforms that give your brand an advanced level of visibility and authority, which will ultimately lead to more media coverage as well. However, just appearing on these platforms is only the beginning.

For example, if you're featured on *Good Morning America*, but your brand identity isn't where it needs to be or you do not have products, services, or experiences to keep people engaged when they go to your website or socials, then you are not in a position to maximize that visibility.

A publicist could possibly land you on some of the biggest shows and media outlets in the world, but if you don't have a brand-building strategy behind your appearance and you do not know where you are going and who you want to reach, you won't be able to maximize these appearances. Typically, a publicist does not help you build your brand; their job is just to help you land media spots, so you will have to do the work of building and engaging with the brand yourself. Agencies will be more full service; however, I have never worked with a media agency. That is why this book spends a great deal of time teaching academics how to go on a journey of brand building. After all, if you get more visibility but do not have ways to monetize that visibility, then you are not on the path to protecting your future outside of the walls of academia.

LANDING A TEDx TALK

The TEDx talk platform leads many academics to secure major book deals, increase speaking fees, and achieve incredible visibility. Of course, after teaching you the tools to land a TEDx talk (and the difference between TEDx and TED), we'll then come full circle to discuss what you need to do after your TEDx talk is public (some of which this book has already addressed).

A TEDx talk may be on your bucket list, and I'm here to tell you that it is possible. And luckily for you, I am going to give you a method that you can implement, not once, but over and over again, to finally land your dream of being on the TEDx stage and delivering an idea worth spreading.

TED VS. TEDX

What's the difference between a TED Talk and a TEDx talk? The simple answer is that a TED Talk is typically done at the main TED event. A TEDx event is a locally organized event that is independent of the TED conference. If you do a good job on your TEDx talk, it might get picked up on the ted.com website (like mine is), or you may be officially invited to present at the main TED conference. By the way, TED stands for Technology, Entertainment, and Design.

Be Proactive

If you have done even a little bit of research into giving a TED Talk, you know that on the main page (ted.com) there's a form where you can nominate someone to give a talk. You can get someone to nominate you or you can nominate yourself, but trying to land a TED Talk this way is like leaving your chances up to luck, because as most of you know, filling out a form on a website usually leads to it being lost in the ether, never to be found again.

You're most likely not going to get a response if you fill out the nomination form on ted.com. I don't believe in leaving things up to chance; I believe in doing things that can possibly lead to reaching your goals. The method I am going to teach you is about minimizing luck and maximizing the strategy that you can use to get on the TED or TEDx stage. Now, of course, if you're reading this, you're going to have a different background, history, credibility, and idea, so for some, this method might takes years, and for others this method might take days. It took me less than five days to land my TEDx talk. And I have found that there are three things you need to keep in mind before you pitch yourself to TED:

- You need to have an idea worth spreading via TED conferences.
- You need to do the branding work that you've learned in this book BEFORE trying to land your TEDx talk.
- You need to make sure the topic you want to present is something you are going to stand by for the rest of your life.

These points are extremely important—they're so important that I'm going to explain each of them in a bit of detail before going over the method of landing a TEDx talk.

Believe Your Idea Is Worth Spreading

Sometimes what we want to do and the timing might not match. For example, I've always wanted to do a TED Talk, but when I was invited the first time to do a TEDx talk, I declined the offer. Why? Because I wasn't ready.

I so often see clients coming to me in a panic because they've gone on media outlets like CNN and aren't happy with their appearance, or they did a TED Talk and are embarrassed by it years later. **It's because they jumped at an opportunity that wasn't right for them because they weren't ready and because they hadn't done the work to create a vision or brand statement.** There was no lens through which to filter opportunities.

Once you do a TEDx talk, you cannot take it back. It will follow you for the rest of your life. It may go viral; you may be offered book deals based on that topic or receive any number of major offers and results. Imagine being famous for something you aren't proud of or can't stand behind.

The best way to avoid these pitfalls is to choose an idea that is based on your area of expertise and/or something that is timeless in your opinion yet meaningful to you. If I had delivered a TEDx talk when I was invited, I would have been creating an idea simply because I was invited. Instead, when I ultimately delivered my talk, I was inspired by an idea first, and then I pitched myself to TED.

The idea that I landed on was something that I knew deep down was important. It felt right. I knew it was the right topic and the right time to then pitch my idea.

The TED model works with topics that you can turn into engaging stories that will bring data and your main point to life. As you're thinking about your idea for your talk, it should be connected with you personally in some way, and you should be able to incorporate moving and emotionally engaging stories into the talk.

My Story

If you look up my TEDx talk, it is called *The Three Self-Empowerment Truths That Will Set You Free,* and in it, I explain these three truths with personal stories and statistics. When viewing my TEDx talk, you might notice that my area of expertise and research on media representation, specific comics, is not what my TEDx talk is about. The main idea of my talk has nothing to do with my research area. I bring this up because while many TED talks are directly related to an individual's research, that doesn't always have to be the case. For me, I had successfully escaped an abusive relationship, and I found myself at a difficult point in my life both during and after that relationship. However, I was able to come out of that situation better and stronger, and thus, my talk was directly related to that experience. (I did get to speak some about my comics writing career, which is on brand.)

I want to give some context on how I discovered my TEDx topic idea, as I believe the thesis of your talk is the hardest part of the process.

When my topic came to me, I was driving in my car and listening to a TEDx talk that my creative coach, Will Toms, delivered, and it hit me like a ton of bricks. I believe that if you give yourself space and time, the topic of your talk will come to you when you're ready.

Then, you will know it is the right time to pitch yourself to TED. And while my topic isn't related to my area of research or expertise, it is directly in line with my brand statement: *I create experiences for free thinkers to feel empowered when they're challenging the status quo.*

This is why your brand statement, identity, and archetype play a major role in all aspects of your brand positioning. Within my TEDx talk, I was able to present information about some of my comic book writing, and the presentation mirrors my career as a creative writer as I incorporated elements of storytelling into the development of the talk. I am sharing this with you to help you get the juices flowing around the possibilities of ideas you can create that are "worth spreading."

My advice to you would be to listen to other TEDx talks, some in the area you are interested in speaking on and others that have nothing to do with your research or area of interest. Find ways to get inspired to come up with a topic that you can connect to personal stories you are comfortable sharing.

Visibility and Impact

While it is exciting to get invited to deliver a TEDx talk, the end result of how you got there really doesn't matter. Whether you were invited or you pitched yourself, it doesn't make a difference to those who are watching your talk at the conference or on YouTube. The goal of delivering a TED or TEDx talk should be because you have something important you want to say, and you want to make the world a better place in whatever way you can. The TED stage is one way to do that.

Just like I teach in my public speaking courses, giving a speech is not about you, it's about the people who are on the receiving end of your words. This is important because imagine doing a TEDx talk and only one hundred people view it. That means you aren't making the type of impact you should with your important idea.

Thus, doing the branding work we've discussed in this book will help you promote your talk to the right people at the right time. Your talk isn't for everyone—just like your brand isn't for everyone. While you might want your talk to be for everybody, as we've already discussed, no product is for every person, and if you try to make everyone happy, you will end up making no one happy—including yourself.

I've worked with a number of clients who have delivered TEDx talks and were under the impression that once it went live, thousands of people would automatically flock to their YouTube pages. That is not the case. The internet is huge, with thousands of TEDx talks online at this point. You need to engage in various activities to put your talk in a position to go viral or get traction. One of those things has to do with the venue itself and where you give the TEDx talk. The other factors have to do with following the blueprint in this book to increase your visibility, authority, and income.

Finally, I want to bring the point home that if you do a TEDx talk and someone lands on your video and likes what you have to say, they will most likely want to know more about you. They will Google you, look up your socials, and try to learn more about you via the internet. You need to control, as much as you can, what they will find when they Google you.

That is why building a brand must be intentional and not haphazard. Imagine someone watching your TEDx talk, then Googling you, and very little comes up, or worse, negative or irrelevant information comes up. Also, if they do get to your web page and socials and they don't find consistent posting or content, then you've lost a potential fan and client. They basically reach a dead end, and you have lost the possibility of gaining another true fan.

This is why you want to keep your website up to date and make sure that your website is "sticky." A sticky website means that when someone lands on it, there are things they can do, and you can keep them on your site for longer periods of time. Ultimately, from your website, they can further engage with you, buy from you, or do things like join your mailing list.

Your TEDx Talk Lives Forever

Your TEDx topic ties into lots of things I've already shared with you; however, this is worth doubling down on. I have a client who went on a major news outlet because she was invited as a guest around a controversial topic. She went on the show because it has worldwide reach; however, what she was going to talk about was a controversial issue that had nothing to do with her area of expertise. She called me in a bit of a frenzy because now this segment has been viewed by millions, and she can't take it back.

This returns us to going viral for something you aren't proud of it. A large part of this book is helping you avoid something like this from happening. What my client should have done was decline the offer and tell the producer that she'd be happy to talk about an area related to her expertise. She could have then pitched that same producer on a different topic later. All media invitations are not in your best interest.

I had to learn this the hard way as well. I say all of this to bring home the point that a TEDx talk will be online and available, most likely, for the rest of your life. So you want to pick a topic with care and deliver a speech with the mindset that it is something you'd be proud to show your great-great-grandkids.

THE FIVE-STEP STRATEGY TO LANDING A TEDX TALK

Without further ado, let me take you through the five-step strategy to landing a TEDx talk. And I can't wait to see some of you on the main ted.com page as well as presenting at the conference!

Step 1: Find an Idea Worth Spreading

The first step in this system involves having the right idea and making sure your online branding is tight. As stated, you need to have an idea worth spreading.

In my opinion, the best way to think about your topic is through the lens of the movie *Pay It Forward*. The main character in the film is a young boy who creates a system to help people. His idea is to help others and then have them help three more people by doing a favor that doesn't require the person to be paid back. Without giving away too much of the movie, the young boy starts a mass movement called Pay It Forward, thus changing the world. This is an example of an idea worth spreading.

Step 2: Create Engaging Video Content of You Speaking

The second step is to get on the speaking engagement circuit or to at least have enough content online that gives the impression that you are a great speaker. If you don't already have speaking engagements in your background, you need to start giving talks or recording videos to post online in an area of your expertise. You can release short educational Instagram videos (which you should be doing anyway as a part of your brand), or you can upload great content of you speaking on YouTube. The point of this is to make sure that once we get to the pitching stage of actually emailing TEDx coordinators and they look you up, there is enough visual material to show them that you are a great speaker and would make a great TEDx speaker at their event.

In addition, doing speaking engagements or public appearances in front of an audience will help you to test out your final TEDx idea. It will help you shape your idea and the signature speech that you will ultimately deliver on the TEDx stage.

But more importantly, you want to at least have one high-quality video of one of your talks online, because this is something that you're going to have to share when you pitch yourself to a TEDx coordinator. Getting on the speaking engagement circuit and having some presentations under your belt is going to help you.

So far, the first two steps are about building social proof and credibility and becoming an authority on whatever it is that you're an expert in. This leads to the third step.

Step 3: Build Your Platform

The third step is amplifying your platform and your voice. You should get some major media coverage and visibility for yourself and your work before you pitch yourself to TEDx.

When I pitched myself to TEDx, I had already been featured in the *Washington Post*, *LA Times*, and beyond. While this level of media coverage and visibility is not required, it certainly helps.

Use the activities and information in this book to grow your media coverage and visibility before pitching yourself to TED.

These first three steps are important because when you're pitching to a TEDx organizer, they most likely do not know you at all and they're going to look you up. Imagine the difference in response between someone who has a fabulous online presence with some major media spots and someone who has very little to show online. Who do you think will get the best response?

Step 4: Identify a Local TEDx Organizer

Go to www.ted.com/TEDx/events (this is the URL as of today). This page shows you all of the TEDx events around the world, when those events are coming up, and where they are.

Depending on how far you're willing to travel, your options may be a little less local. For example, since I am in Philadelphia, I searched the site for TEDx events around Philadelphia. I might be willing to travel to Delaware or New York, so I can expand my search out to those states. However, for me, I only focused on Philadelphia first.

I recommend starting your search as local as possible. Each of the TEDx events that come up will list an organizer or organizers. Most of the time, when you click on the organizer's name or profile, it will take you to another page, but the page rarely lists direct contact information.

If it has a direct email address, you now have a person to send your pitch materials to. However, that is not the case most of the time.

You may have to do a little internet research on your own to narrow down the person's email address or Facebook or X page to send them a message. Preferably, you want their email address. This might take a few minutes to a few days. Some organizers will be easier to find than others. However, once you narrow down that contact information for at least one or two event organizers, it's time to move on to the fifth and final step.

Step 5: Make Your Pitch

Email or message the organizers and make your pitch. It's likely they receive pitches from lots of people, so when you email them, there are some things you want to do to stand out. Briefly tell them about your idea and how you use it to help or inspire people. You want to do this in two to three sentences. For example:

> Hi, Kathy,
>
> My name is Dr. Jane Doe. I see you're the organizer of the Burn Library TEDx event. I am interested in speaking at the event, and I've been featured in the *LA Times* and the *Washington Post* for my work around XYZ. I have a TEDx idea called XYX.

Describe your TEDx idea, tell the organizer why you think the topic is important in today's world, and attach your electronic press kit (EPK). You can create an EPK on freelancing sites such as Fiverr.com.

Now, you might have to email a few different people; however, if you do not get a response after a few days, always follow up. These are real people with real lives. Their full-time job is not organizing TEDx talks, so sometimes people may miss your email or just forget to respond. Success is in the follow-up, as detailed with media appearances in the previous chapter.

While others may teach different ways of landing a TED or TEDx talk, and while even TEDx itself will say these things are not required, what we're doing is minimizing luck and maximizing strategy. At this point, you might be thinking that these steps are not something that you can do today. If you haven't established a presence or strong brand and you do not have a topic you believe in, maybe it's true, and you're just not there yet.

You'll know when you feel like you're there; you'll know when your platform is built up enough and you believe you have a voice and credibility around your brand. You'll know when you feel like you have enough speaking engagements under your belt, and you have high-quality links to your speaking engagements. You'll know when you have an idea worth spreading. You will know. It's just a matter of being honest with yourself and taking the time to work through these steps.

So, as with media events, build up your voice and platform (as discussed in the previous chapter) using the tools and techniques offered in this book before you pitch a TEDx organizer. Do op-eds in major and local news outlets and blog outlets, secure media spots, and get feature pieces written about you. These are strongly suggested prerequisites before moving on to the next step.

And when do you land a TEDx talk, you've already exponentially increased your chances of getting on the main TED stage. After your talk, you're going to want to create buzz around it. You're going to want to share that on your social media platforms and use some boost posts (FB ads) and other paid advertisement sites to get more traction and visibility.

BOOSTING POSTS

Boosting a post on Facebook means paying to promote a regular post from your page to a wider audience. It increases the post's visibility beyond your followers and allows you to reach a larger audience. People boost posts to expand their reach, target specific demographics, promote updates or events, drive website traffic, and increase brand awareness. However, it's important to note that boosting a post doesn't guarantee conversions or long-term engagement; it's simply a tool to amplify your content on Facebook. This feature may be available on other social media platforms as well.

GET YOUR BOOKS INTO BRICK AND MORTAR STORES

In this new world where anyone can publish a book on Amazon, getting your book published by a book publisher and having it appear in a brick-and-mortar store will set you apart from others. It will convey status and do wonders for your credibility and authority.

I want to take a moment here to let you know that the method I am teaching you doesn't involve utilizing a literary agent. There are two reasons for that. First, I've never used a literary agent, and I only believe in teaching people how to do things I have actually done myself. Second, any article on the internet is going to tell you that publishing with a traditional publisher involves getting an agent.

Most people I work with think that they need an agent to get their book on the shelves of places like Barnes & Noble and other bookstore chains. But there are other ways to reach your goals that have worked for me and tons of my clients. I've had success with this method, and I know it works. Ultimately, though, you may decide to retain an agent.

I tell my clients that they should seek to publish their academic book with an independent publisher with a track record of getting books into bookstores. Bookstores still have an advantage in the minds of many consumers because:

- They give customers a chance to try out items before buying them. Some people still like physically flipping through the entirety of a book while browsing the bookstore.
- They offer customers an opportunity for immediate pleasure with their new book purchases in hand.
- They create a personal connection with their patrons. Some people like checking out their book at the register and feeling as though they are supporting their local bookstore.

And don't get me wrong—people have been highly successful self-publishing their books. In fact, at the time of writing this book, I have self-published three of my own. One of them was even featured in *Good Morning America* digital, and another one has distribution in a large grocery store chain. But for the most part, a self-published book is not going to end up on the shelf of a bookstore unless you physically go to the store and ask to place it there.

I've had numerous books land in brick-and-mortar stores, everything from comic books to my academics books, and it's a nice surprise to be in a bookstore as far away from the States as Australia and see your book there. At the time of writing this book, I have never had an agent, and I have published at least one book a year every year since 2014 (not including comic book issues for Marvel and DC comics or books I've written for clients). Therefore, you absolutely do not need to have an agent to follow the method I am laying out.

Find Aligned Publishers

The first thing you'll want to do is publish your work through a publisher, but not just any publisher. Before you even write your book, you need to be strategic. Take a trip to Barnes & Noble or the local bookstore closest to you. Look for the section in the store that has books similar to the one you will write.

Once you've identified the section that your book would be in, you're going to conduct some research. Pull fifteen books from that section and open to the copyright page of each. Write down the publisher's name for each book. Ideally, you'll have fifteen different publishers' names on this sheet of paper, but most likely you will not. You might have fewer because some books might be from the same publisher.

Research Submission Guidelines

Now it's time to do some research. You will be happy to learn that there are lots of smaller independent presses that don't require an agent.

Go to the submission page of each book publisher you've found and research their criteria for submitting a proposal. Most publishers have proposal guidelines and contact information for who to send your proposal to. From your list, cross off all of the publishing houses that require an agent. When you're ready to pitch your book, you will need a proposal and at least one sample chapter. The quality of your proposal matters as much as the strength of your online presence when submitting. Note that at this point, you do not need a fully written book. You'll flesh it out once you're signed up.

The Most Important Question to Ask

If you get a contract offer, one of the most important questions to ask during the process is: *What's your marketing strategy or plan for getting my book into brick-and-mortar stores?*

You'll want to make sure they have a strategy and a history of getting books into stores. There are never any guarantees, but the process here maximizes strategy and minimizes luck.

In this chapter, you learned how to elevate your credibility and authority by having a laser-focused strategy to access platforms that increase your visibility. While we focused on landing a TEDx talk and getting your books into brick-and-mortar stores, there are countless (specifically in-person) platforms that may be right for you. With what you've learned, I'd love to see you devise a plan to get the ball moving on accessing your ideal platforms, whether it's sending emails to the right people, researching who runs specific platforms, and/or mailing out your EPK to key leaders of that platform. Get started!

Also, please remember that landing a TED Talk, getting your book in bookstores, and accessing other high-level platforms are not easy goals. They require a significant amount of preparation and effort. Academics who wish to deliver a successful TEDx talk or access that platform that is major to their field must be able to distill their research and ideas into a compelling and engaging narrative that resonates with that specific platform's audience and/or stakeholders.

In addition, visibility allows more people to discover who you are and what you have to offer, which gives you a chance to further engage with new fans and followers on a more personal level when they seek you on social media. Combining consistent media coverage with steady and strategic visibility will have a snowball effect that you can then use for more social media content. It becomes a nice cycle for increasing your visibility and authority.

PART III

Capital

CHAPTER 8

1,000 True Fans

ongrats on all of the work you've done so far. You are now in phase three of the Power Your Research process, which is monetization. Here we will cover the mechanics of turning your brand into a six-figure business and then move on to creating a sales funnel for your services and products.

If you haven't read and executed what you've learned in the book so far, it's important that you do so before jumping into trying to monetize. You can't sell anything to anyone consistently if you do not know who you are, who your audience is, what your audience likes and needs, and all of the other important systems we've discussed so far. There are no shortcuts to success, in spite of all the hype on social media these days around how to make money quickly. It's a process. Trust the process and the tactics needed to make it work for you.

A BRIEF RECAP

In Chapters 1 and 2, we discussed mindset. There are so many key elements around mindset that are important to your success, but one aspect is the community around you. It is not always welcome in academia to talk about making money outside of your faculty or academic position. Simple things like increasing your speaking engagement rate can make other academics turn their noses up at you. The thing to remember is your vision. It is your life, not your colleagues' lives. **If you want to make an impact at scale, you have to do what your colleagues and peers aren't doing.** That means, along your journey, you need to make money to continue to reach more people. Spend time around academics and entrepreneurs who understand and appreciate the market value of your work. This is key as we delve into building capital.

In Chapter 3, you developed your own personal vision. You nailed down why this matters to you and why you have embarked on this journey of building your brand. This is going to be crucial as you build your business financially. Your dreams will take work and require doing things you may not want to do on a daily basis for those dreams to come true. Everything you try to implement around monetization is not going to be effective right away. You have to stick with it. You need to be willing to adjust. You cannot give up on selling your product or service after thirty days. It is your "why" statement that will get you through the tough times and to the other side of increasing your income to six figures.

In Chapter 4, you developed your brand statement, brand archetype, and brand adjectives. You want to remember that the service and/or product you sell should align with your brand statement, and your brand's messaging should align with your brand assets. Let's use Dr. Newland as an example to see how this all works together.

If you remember, Dr. Cynthia Newland is an academic in the DEI and mental health field. Her brand statement is *I create resources for visionaries to feel liberated when they're challenging the status quo.* Her brand archetype is the Rebel. Her brand adjectives are "narrative changer," "visionary," and "trailblazer."

At this point in the Power Your Research process, Dr. Newland has already been getting a trickle of speaking engagements and has a passion for helping mental health agencies better serve families of color. Dr. Newland will lean into monetizing her speaking engagements and creating consistent consulting opportunities to work with well-established mental health agencies that need assistance serving families of color through offering resources, practices, and more effective hiring strategies. She will do this by using her brand as the Rebel, where she will offer ideas and implementation that are highly effective, proven, and progressive. Even if Dr. Newland decides to do something new and write a children's book, she would make sure it fell under the scope of her brand assets.

Chapters 5, 6, and 7 have allowed you to learn about your audience by engaging with them on social media and then getting media coverage and visibility around your area of expertise. This means you are comfortable talking to your audience and building that SEO needed to bring you up on Google searches around your topic. **Therefore, you now have the right factors in place to offer your audience value on a consistent basis in exchange for money.**

With the clarity from Chapters 2 through 7, Dr. Newland can now learn the systems and strategies for creating her six-figure road map. The Power Your Research process will start Dr. Newland off with an understanding of the 1,000 True Fans model and the power of her innovators and early adopters. She will know how to activate her true fans into true income, while serving the audience she cares about the most.

And now, the focus turns a small group of people into customers and the foundation you will need to increase your income.

WHAT IS THE CONCEPT OF 1,000 TRUE FANS?

First introduced by author, editor, and the founding executive editor of *Wired* magazine, Kevin Kelly, in his 2010 book *1,000 True Fans*, the very core of the 1,000 True Fans concept is that every artist or entrepreneur needs to find one thousand people who will purchase anything and everything they produce. So, if you have one thousand people who are willing to buy your work for $100 each, then you will make $100,000 a year using this framework. Within the context of the Diffusion of Innovation theory (page 101), you'll see in this chapter that the 1,000 True Fans concept is powerful when applying these frameworks in tandem.

A "true fan" or "super fan" is someone who buys from you and talks about you or your products in public. (Linking back to the Diffusion of Innovation theory, these will be your innovators and early adopters.) The idea is that you need one thousand of these—you do not need to be a worldwide celebrity to make lots of money from the people who love you. You just need to be a celebrity to a few.

These are people who tell their friends about you, and they are shocked that their friends don't know who you are. "You don't know Dr. _____?" they say. That is what you want your one thousand true fans to say and feel when they mention you to their friends, family, and colleagues.

Getting one thousand fans is much more doable than feeling like you have to reach millions of people to sell your product or service. This concept can be applied in many ways, but the most popular way is to use it as a marketing strategy. This means that you will need to find a thousand people who are willing to buy your product or service. This is not easy, but it is simple.

As we focused on in Chapter 5, when people find you, you want to be able to offer them something that keeps them on your website, engaged with your social media content, and in your network for an extended period of time. Lifetime fans are lifetime financial supporters who love what you have to offer.

That means you always want to have something for people to buy when they do find you, whether it is an online course, a consulting opportunity, coaching, or physical products such as T-shirts. The sky is really the limit as to what you have to offer people, and remember, the paid service or product you are offering needs to align with your brand and offer value to the right people.

So if someone hears you on a podcast, and then they search for you online and there's nothing to buy once they find your website and socials, it's a dead end for a potential customer. Thus, the 1,000 True Fans concept is so useful when it comes to brand building. You are the business, and your brand will attract people to your paid offerings. Make the experience of searching for you worth it for both you and the potential supporter!

A lot of times, we want to focus on the most likes, the most shares, and the most comments on our latest social media post, but really we should be focusing on the people who are already buying from us and talking about us, because if you have one thousand true fans (innovators and early adopters), and all of them spend $100 on you each year, well, you now have a six-figure business. From there, you can scale that base to infinity and beyond, as I like to say.

The great thing about this model is that it is malleable. Is starting out with one hundred true fans more doable for you? Five hundred? Take the time right now to jot down what makes sense for you at this time. I might write, "This year I will serve two hundred true fans and make $200 each." That's $40,000, and that's amazing!

IMPLEMENTING THE 1,000 TRUE FANS CONCEPT: THREE EXAMPLES

As with many of the tactics presented in this book, these examples provide information on implementing this strategy, but I cannot cover each and every scenario out there. For some, you may be able to replicate the steps below, but for others, you will have to use your own discernment based on your brand, what you sell, and who your target audience is. I encourage you to jot down notes and ideas as you learn, so you can experiment with what might work for your specific situation and get new ideas for finding your true fans. And as you experiment and execute, use the methods and tactics that work best for your specific situation.

In Chapter 5: "Social Media Strategy," we used Bob as an example of what it might look like to turn someone into a true fan who has engaged with us on Instagram. (By following the social media strategy laid out in this book, you have already been implementing parts of the 1,000 True Fans model without even knowing it!)

In this section, we will go deeper into how you can find your super fans, keep track of them, and cater to them so they will continue to amplify your work and engage with your brand—whether it be as customers or people who can connect you to other opportunities. (And I want to reiterate the message in Chapter 5 so you remember that the key is to give back to the people who are already paying attention to you so that *they* can spread your message and throw you over to the masses!)

At this point, you still might have the following questions:

1. How do I find more of my super fans?
2. How do I figure out what they want from me?
3. How do I create more super fans?

I had these same questions when I first started out, and there are some easy answers, such as who might be buying one of your digital courses or products and posting a review.

Example #1: Fiverr.com

When starting out on my entrepreneurial journey, one of my streams of income was from the freelance site Fiverr.com. There are a number of sites similar to this, but Fiverr happens to be the one I use most. It is an online platform that connects freelancers with businesses and individuals who need their services. It is a great way for freelancers to make money by offering their services (web design, development, copywriting, marketing, etc.) to clients all over the world. I have relied on Fiverr to help with things my businesses need, and it provides great tools for managing projects, tracking progress, and communicating with clients. I also create gigs on the site, and I mention this because not only do I make money on the site, but it is a great place to find true fans.

CREATING GIGS ON FIVERR.COM

With Fiverr, you can create a gig, set your own rates, and start getting paid. Fiverr makes it easy for freelancers to find work and make money without having to go through the hassle of landing clients on their own. The other side of Fiverr consists of clients who *offer* gigs to freelancers. The site's terminology applies "creating gigs" to the type of work freelancers want to do for those who are looking to hire assistance—clients.

Of course, you need to do research on the type of gig you want to create, and you need to make sure you have the time and skills to deliver the service. I like to create gigs that do not require a lot of my time and that align with my vision.

As of the writing of this book, I have two gigs on Fiverr. One gig is a social media influencer gig, where I promote other people's comic books. For the second gig, I create marketing plans for authors. These gigs combined bring in about $500 to $800 a month. That might not seem like a lot, but combined with other income streams, the money starts adding up.

One beautiful thing about Fiverr is that the platform markets and promotes your gigs for you. It even shows you the click rate on your gig and the number of impressions you are getting monthly. So while Fiverr does take a cut from what you earn, you do not need to spend marketing dollars on promoting your services.

Where to Find the True Fans on Fiverr

This is where using Fiverr starts getting fun.

Clients who hire you through the site can leave reviews once you complete the work for them. If the review is glowing, you now have a potential true fan—a person who has not only paid you, but has talked about you publicly. People from all over the world have found me on Fiverr and ended up hiring me for outside consulting purposes and other highly paid opportunities.

This has allowed me to make so much more money simply because of the exposure and alignment in my product offerings and services. Thus, it is critical that all of the things you do are in alignment and can bounce one customer to other products and services that they can pay you for as well.

For instance, people who are in the comics space find me on Fiverr, and then find out I also have a comics course on Udemy (an education technology company that provides online learning and teaching platform), and from there they might become members of my membership site.

Because all of those things are aligned and serving the same audience, it is like a feedback loop, where I can offer the same type of customer lots of different services to help them tell stories in the comics medium that they care about.

Here's my strategy in a nutshell:

- I ask my clients for reviews after positive interactions.
- I check to see which clients are leaving reviews on my Fiverr gig.
- For those who leave nice reviews, I send a personal message thanking them.
- I let them know that I have free resources on my Instagram page.
- I also point them to my digital courses.

Thus, when someone hires me on Fiverr and leaves a great review, I now have another way to track my super fans. From there, I can engage with them and include them on an Excel spreadsheet (refer back to the importance of documenting in Chapter 5, page 100).

My spreadsheet includes:

- The person's name or social media handle
- Notes about any important comments or suggestions they've made
- Where they bought from me

This allows me to keep them in my feedback loop to serve them more of my other services and products.

This method allows:

1. Me to easily identify my true fans (those who hire me and leave reviews)
2. Me to let my Fiverr clients know that I am available for coaching and consulting calls at a small price (additional offerings to get me to the $100-from-one-thousand-people mark)
3. Fiverr to do the marketing to bring more people into my network

It almost feels like Fiverr is paying me to do my marketing. Are they making good money off the people who are buying my gig? Yes. But it is a mutually beneficial arrangement if I think about all of the other ways I am benefitting. In addition, I am serving and helping people whom I care about, because as a writer, I care about helping people tell their own stories and share their work.

I want to bring home the point that **documenting those who buy from you and talk about you in a spreadsheet is the best way to start implementing the 1,000 True Fans concept.** The reason this needs to be reiterated is because this can be time-consuming and cumbersome, but it is worth it in order to reach your financial goals. Your goal is to get one thousand people documented on that spreadsheet.

Start engaging with them (interacting on social media) and start adding genuine value to their lives. If each of these people spends fifty dollars on you in a year, you have $50,000 in revenue. You can create whatever goal you want around this concept.

For example, starting out, you might say you want to create three hundred super fans and have them spend $150 on you in one calendar year. That means you'd have a revenue goal of $45,000 for the year. Implementing a system where your client has multiple avenues to buy from you makes this completely doable without much overhead expense. And this is just the beginning in terms of monetization!

Example #2: Social Media

Here's another method that might work for you to figure out who your true fans are.

Most people have one or two social media sites that they feel more comfortable using. For a long time, it was X for me. I'm a writer, so naturally, X was easy for me. I was able to do well by posting regularly and eventually getting verified on the platform (before you could pay for verification). This greatly helped boost my followership. If you're trying to figure out where to start with the social media platform you use to reach your audience, begin with the platform you've historically been posting on the most. From there, you can implement the following process to find your true fans:

- Comb through your posts, comments, and direct messages to identify those who have left positive messages about your books or products in the past.

- If you haven't sold anything yet, make it a plan to figure out the ways in which you can monetize your platform of choice. Start with things you enjoy doing as well as things you are good at.*
- Once you begin offering products and services and talking about them on social media, people will buy. Ask them for feedback or reviews of their experience or of your product, and once those reviews begin to come in, you have your first round of true fans.
- When you identify those from your past social media posts, comments, and DMs who have bought from you and tweeted you or responded to a social media message positively, you want to include those people on an Excel spreadsheet. They are true fans.
- You want to segment your audiences when necessary. For example, my academic branding audience is on a different social media platform (LinkedIn) than the audience who wants to hear about comic books and graphic novels (Instagram). I also segment them in my mailing list system (I use Mailchimp and ActiveCampaign), keeping those two audiences separate. If you have more than one business or type of customer that you are selling to, keep these target audiences on separate Excel sheets.

---

* My accountant shared some transformational advice with me when we first met. He said that if you want to make money, do something you're good at. Lots of us are following passions, and while I believe in following your passion, I also coach clients to find ways to pair their passions with what they are good at. My company Power Your Research blends my love of marketing (something I am great at) with teaching (something I like and do well). This allows me to make money by doing something that blends both my passion and the things I am good at.

Example #3: Teachable

Teachable.com is a platform where you can host online courses. It is different from Udemy in that it does not do the marketing for you. Every aspect of marketing is totally on you, the course creator. However, the benefit of this is that you can make more money on your courses, as the platform does not take such a big cut compared to Udemy.

For example, if I have a course on teachable for $100, I will bring home around $85 after fees. For my teachable courses, I add "upsells," which are things you can sell customers when they buy one course.

So, if they are buying a $50 course on how to earn extra money as a comics creator, I can provide a button to allow them to add on an additional class for $50. That's called an upsell, and with this method, you can configure the customer journey in a way that will get you to the $100 mark quicker.

Using a platform like Teachable, you also have greater access to your students. So you can connect Teachable to your mailing list, where you can then offer your students more value by sending an email each month. Your mailing list might offer lots of free content and some paid content, increasing your ability to sell your customers—who already love what you are offering.

Documenting people who love you will allow you to check in with them and get to know them, thus allowing you to figure out more of their psychographics and what they like. Interacting with your true fans is key to getting to know them. They will start telling you exactly what they want.

As you can see, with a little creativity, there are hundreds of ways to make one person a $100 customer. By implementing the intentional tools in these examples, you will spend the next year engaging with your audience and identifying more and more true fans. (Don't forget to create that spreadsheet!)

And the sky is the limit here, as the 1,000 True Fans concept allows you to scale up each year. Once you have perfected creating $100-a-year customers, you can increase that to turning one thousand fans into $200-a-year customers, and so on and so forth.

Obviously, this is not a get-rich-quick formula. All of this requires time and effort on your part. Once you begin the process of documenting your true fans, most of you will see, as I did, that it takes work to get one thousand true fans. However, the good news is that all of us already have a few, no matter where our starting point is. If you're selling something or have a product or a book, even if it is a book from an academic publisher, someone has bought it, and someone has said they like it (whether online or to you personally).

Of course, we have to put out quality material that our fans like. When you truly understand the Diffusion of Innovation theory (page 101) coupled with the 1,000 True Fans concept, it becomes clear how you can start a mass movement, beginning with a few and growing to many.

CHAPTER 9

The Sales Funnel

Now it is time to go deeper into sales. The 1,000 True Fans model will get you far, but understanding the pathway to making someone a customer will allow you to create consistent income and scale beyond $100,000. The 1,000 True Fans model is the foundation from which you can grow substantially once it is combined with the skill set of building a sales funnel.

If you've successfully made money using the techniques learned in the 1,000 True Fans chapter, then you have actually already created a sales funnel. A sales funnel is the representation of the steps someone takes to become a customer. That might be someone buying your book, hiring you as a consultant, booking a coaching call, or paying you to do a speaking engagement.

Sales funnels help you keep a particular income stream consistent, and they allow you to understand where your potential customers are in the buying journey. With a good sales funnel, you can begin to predict critical information like how many customers you will get each month or how many leads you need to get each month in order to make a certain amount of money on a consistent basis.

While the 1,000 True Fans concept can get you to six figures, the content in this chapter will help you understand the power of a system and the buyer's journey so that you can better project your revenue.

As you learn about sales funnels, take notes on how you can create one for the items, products, or services you have chosen to monetize. After we take a deep dive into the stages of a sales funnel, we will apply these stages to speaking engagements (something every academic can relate to). I consider speaking engagements low-hanging fruit, as they are something you can build off of to start significantly monetizing right away.

THE SALES FUNNEL: DEEP DIVE

"Sales funnel" is the marketing term for the journey a consumer takes from being completely unfamiliar with you to buying your product. As the name implies, it's designed to funnel the target audience toward taking your desired action.

The typical sales funnel has four stages:

1. Awareness
2. Interest
3. Desire
4. Action

As you learn this new information, think about how you can apply this to your income vehicles—whether that's generating consistent speaking engagements, book sales, coaching, digital courses, and so on. I will provide various examples and the ways in which I think about sales funnels because it is critical to creating a profitable brand. Without a sales funnel, you cannot grow at scale.

The diagram below reflects the stages of the sales funnel that this chapter covers.

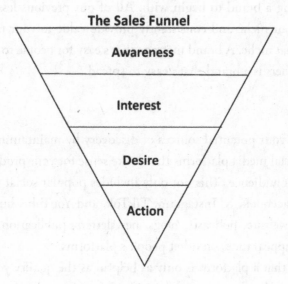

The Sales Funnel

Awareness

Interest

Desire

Action

Stage 1: Awareness

The awareness stage is when the potential customer realizes that a seller is offering a product or service that fits their needs. In a narrow sense, our target audience's awareness stage begins when they receive word that you are offering something of potential value. In a broader sense, however, we don't want to settle here.

Our larger goal is not just awareness that we are currently selling something but brand recognition in general. Consider all of the largest brands in the world, such as Coca-Cola, Apple, McDonald's, and Google. Do these brands have to market directly to you in order for you to know that they are currently offering products that they would like you to buy? I doubt it. These brands have all built sources to generate passive brand awareness, from word of mouth and media coverage to simple ubiquity—being present absolutely everywhere you look.

Define Your Niche

The most important step to building brand awareness for yourself is first having a brand to begin with. All of our previous lessons apply: Define your niche and consistently provide value to your target audience in that niche. A brand message that's easy for people to communicate to others is a brand that's easy to spread.

Diversify

Diversify your potential sources of discovery by maintaining presence on the social media platforms that make sense for your product/service and target audience. This not only includes popular social media sites such as Facebook, X, Instagram, TikTok, and YouTube, but also your personal website, podcasts, blogs, newsletters, publications, advertising, and appearances on other people's platforms.

Note that a platform is only as helpful as the quality you put into it. A personal website that gets you in front of people's eyes but turns them off from moving further down the sales funnel is not helping you. So when adding a new platform to your arsenal, take some time to make sure that it is communicating your brand effectively and that it demonstrates thought and care.

Network

Networking can also be a boon to spreading brand awareness. Meeting new contacts and building your stable of potential leads can ensure that even if you are competing with many other people for your niche in the broader market, those contacts are still likely to think of you first when that niche comes up because they have a personal connection with you.

Employ Unofficial Brand Ambassadors

People you are connected to are considered hot or warm audiences, and as we move forward, we will delve deeper into how to effectively activate them. For right now, though, you just need to know that hot or warm audiences are people who already know about you and your offerings, and cold audiences are people who do not know about you or your offerings. What's more, contacts who are familiar with you can themselves become unofficial brand ambassadors for you, spreading the word of your work, your credibility, and your expertise.

And if those contacts have their own platforms, you may have an opportunity to be featured on those mediums and get exposure to a new audience.

For example, though there are many brilliant people working on Black comics and the scholarship regarding them, the people on my list of hot and warm audience members are likely to think of me first if the topic comes up, as I may be the only connection they have to the topic.

Then, since my warm and hot audience members are all connected with higher education institutions, they may be able to make other people in their departments aware of my work on Black comics history and my own comics and therefore help me build brand awareness. They also likely have many other higher education professionals in their social network, so if they share my book *Encyclopedia of Black Comics* on their X feed, many other people in my target audience are likely to see it and become aware of my work.

Create Clear Steps in Your Funnel

Finally, since building awareness is about casting a wide net, we want to make sure that the people who come across you casually can move further down the funnel with as little work as possible, especially if they are in your target audience.

To that end, there must be clear steps interested people can take to find more information and move deeper down the funnel, and it must be available within a few clicks.

If you are posting on social media, make sure that your contact information or links to purchase your services are in your bio. If you are on a podcast, make sure your social media is shared in the description. If the prospective customer is able to easily access more information after becoming aware of you, they will move on to the interest stage.

Stage 2: Interest

The interest stage is where the potential customer expresses a curiosity about the product or service and begins evaluating it and comparing it to your competitors to decide whether or not they would like to buy it.

At this stage, your goal as a seller is to build brand trust and make a compelling case why the buyer should choose you over competitors. This boils down to our friend, social proof (see page 106).

To make the case for yourself, your brand, and your services, you need to be able to show that you can fill a customer's needs, that you are the best choice, and that the customer will have no regrets upon choosing you.

The benefit of establishing ourselves in a narrow niche and choosing narrow and specific topics is that we are only committed to filling a narrow range of needs, and our credibility and authority only has to prove that we are capable of filling that finite set of needs.

For example, if your brand is that you help STEM schools and organizations address blind spots in their recruitment, education, or employment of women, you do not need to also prove that you can help them reduce their carbon footprint. You only need to show that discrimination against and underrepresentation of women is a problem in STEM, that this is a problem worth addressing for your prospective customer, and that you are able to help them do so.

If you are able to show the customer that they have a need that isn't being met and then prove you are the person to fill that need, the next stop is desire.

Stage 3: Desire

In the desire stage, the potential customer wants your product or service and believes it will fill their need. They have been convinced of the product or service's efficacy, but they haven't yet taken the action to purchase it.

A good analogy from the world of online shopping is that the desire stage is like adding a product to the cart but not yet completing the purchase. At this stage, the seller's goals are to explain why the product or information you are offering is important right now and to be transparent about what you are offering and how it will benefit the prospect.

For example, there are often news stories about STEM organizations systematically treating women poorly or creating unwelcoming environments for them (such as the story from a few years ago about some Google employees saying that the underrepresentation of women at Google was due to women being biologically less predisposed to working in technology), and avoiding falling prey to those same pitfalls is a great opportunity that many organizations would jump at.

Even if your topics are not in the news, consider whether they reflect recent breakthroughs in research, complement national holidays or events, or are particularly useful at a certain time of year. Students may find tips for self-care and mental health maintenance especially useful at the beginning of the semester, for example, as they can then focus on these tips before their workload becomes overwhelming and put them into practice throughout the upcoming semester.

Some products and services have a seasonality to them. This means, at certain times of the year, your audience might be triggered to buy what you offer due to external factors.

For example, in Philadelphia, the water ice shops are only open during the summer. Thus, if you are from Philadelphia, the summer triggers a desire for water ice (known as "Italian ices" or "slush" in nearby states) if you are into cold treats. Or those who work in the mental health field might see an uptick in clients and interest when Mental Health Awareness Month comes around. Therefore, you can plan to build off the desire to seek out mental health treatment during this time in order to get your product or service in front of more people.

At this stage, as you share information regarding the benefit and features of your services, you may feel the inclination to offer more or lower your prices to coax the prospective customer into taking action. **There is a time and a place for going out of your way to do more or ask for less compensation, but I encourage you to make valuing your own time and experience a priority.** Rather than devaluing your work, try to encourage the customer into action by explaining the importance and benefits of the work you are doing. If the customer believes the product or service you offer is worth the compensation you ask for, they are sure to take action. Give people value. That is how you turn someone's desire into the action of buying, which is the next stage.

Stage 4: Action

The fourth and final stage is the action stage—where the desired execution is taken, money changes hands, and the prospective customer becomes an actual customer.

Once the customer has been brought to this point, the seller's goal is simply to get out of their own way. When the customer has decided to take the desired action—whether that is booking you for a consulting job or speaking engagement, airing your film, hiring you for one-on-one coaching, or anything else—you want to make that action as effortless for them as possible. This is the time to provide value.

There is a reason Amazon offers one-click purchasing; consider how much Amazon sales would drop if you had to click multiple buttons to complete a purchase. Take a page out of Amazon's book in this regard and provide a clear method for customers to complete the transaction or contact you, and make sure they have any and all information they will need to do so.

———————

Our ultimate goal is to set up a sales funnel that will passively generate interest from parties looking to pay us for high-paid opportunities and convince them to take the leap with minimal intervention from us. Master the fundamentals above and you'll have speaking engagements and other paid opportunities pouring in. The great news is that at this point in the Power Your Research process, you have already been implementing some of these strategies in your social media content.

The next section will give you some initial, concrete steps to take in order to get started with creating your sales funnel.

TAKE THE FIRST THREE STEPS

Here are some concrete action items to consider in starting the sales funnel process.

Step 1: Brand Awareness

For our first step, I want you to incorporate some brand awareness activities into your daily schedule, if you haven't already done so. As discussed, you need to amplify getting your personal academic brand in front of more people and more of the right people (awareness stage). You should rely on your area(s) of expertise as well as what you are monetizing to narrow down who your audience is and the types of people/organizations you want to connect with.

Here's a list (not exhaustive) of possible things you can be doing in the brand awareness stage, and you can use any of these items as a place to begin:

- Post on social media three to four times a day through the lens of your brand assets.
- Post short-form and long-form educational videos on social media platforms as well as your blog.
- Go to networking events and meet people inside and outside of your field.
- Engage with others at local co-working spaces both inside and outside of your field.
- Set up video meetings with entrepreneurs both inside and outside of your field.
- Write op-eds across various platforms around your area(s) of expertise for a mass audience.
- Write new content on your personal blog and sites such as medium.com or similar.
- Consider using a site like Blip to buy cheap billboards in major cities.
- Do Instagram live broadcasts on other people's pages in your area of expertise.
- Use LinkedIn sales navigator to introduce yourself to individuals and organizations in your area(s) of expertise.
- Appear on major platforms like TEDx and Ted stages.
- Send an email every six months letting colleagues know that you are open for speaking engagements and consultantships.

The key is to identify what works for you and then to be consistent with whatever activities you choose.

Step 2: Brand Trust and Credibility

The second step I want you to take is to incorporate some brand trust and credibility activities into your daily schedule and output. These activities should be in alignment with the interest phase of the sales funnel.

Remember, the ultimate goal of the interest stage is to move the potential customer closer to making a purchase by building trust, demonstrating value, and establishing a relationship. It is important to provide clear and concise information that helps the potential customer make an informed decision about whether your product or service is the right fit for them. You can also reengage past customers or clients with brand interest activities. These activities might include:

- Sending short thank-you cards to venues or colleagues who have supported you over the last year (this builds a relationship).
- Making sure you are posting educational, useful content at least once a day on your socials (this adds value and clarifies what you offer).
- Staying in contact with colleagues and your network by inviting people to brief check-in meetings, where you remind them of your products/services.
- Getting social proof and posting it online. Post client testimonials and workshop testimonials (this builds trust).
- Reposting positive book reviews on your socials (this builds credibility).

Step 3: Turn People into Customers

The third and final step I want you to take is to incorporate some activities that can turn people into customers. These might include:

- Sharing your purchase link two to three times a day for one week.
- Asking people who are interested in your program to DM you to learn more, and when they engage, send them your purchase link.
- Experimenting with two different Facebook ads at five dollars a day to see which ad results in link clicks. Analyze the data to see which one worked best.

- Reaching out to the true fans you have identified and asking them what they need help with. When they reply, offer a solution to their problem through one of your paid programs.
- Inviting your target audience to a free thirty-minute discovery call, and then, on the call, taking them through how you can help them and offering your product/service.

In the next section, we will apply the stages of sales funnels to speaking engagements. You will learn the Power Your Research process for generating consistent speaking engagement opportunities by utilizing the stages of a sales funnel.

THE SALES FUNNEL AND SPEAKING ENGAGEMENTS

High-paid speaking engagement opportunities may seem unattainable, but as someone with an advanced degree, you already have everything you need to take your first step to start charging at least $3,500 for a one-hour talk.

The recipe you'll use to kickstart and maintain this process has three simple ingredients:

- The topic
- The target
- The pitch

Together, these three ingredients form the foundation of your sales funnel—the journey your potential customers take from never having heard of you to booking you to speak to an audience.

Ingredient 1: The Topic

The first step to any speaking engagement is the topic. If you want to speak to a large group of people, you must talk to them about something, and the subject will often help determine the appropriate audience.

A good topic is the confluence of three things: credibility, area of expertise, and what you want to talk about.

Credibility

Credibility is all about trust. The event organizers need to be able to trust that if they give you a platform to speak to an audience, the information you will share with them is accurate, and the listeners will walk away having had a good experience.

Demonstrating credibility is similar to social proof. You must show that you have a proven track record of concrete, measurable successes in your chosen topic. Luckily, you have a head start here as your advanced degree is a powerful source of credibility. It shows that a group of academic experts have validated your knowledge in the field of your degree.

But if you don't want to speak on your research area, don't despair. There are plenty of other forms of social proof you can lean on. These include awards you have won for your work in a field, interviews or other coverage of your work by established journalistic outlets, collaborations with or testimonials by established experts in the area, demonstrable work you have done on the subject, or previous speaking engagements on the topic.

As a personal example, one topic I might choose to talk about is the legacy of Martin Luther King Jr. I have credibility on this topic because I have taught a class on Martin Luther King's America, I have done previous speaking engagements for Martin Luther King Jr. Day, and I have research publications having to do with African American history. Another example topic for me is the history of Black comic strips, and

I can demonstrate my credibility on the topic because I won an award for a book I wrote about Black comics.

Area of Expertise

An area of expertise is the subject that you have put time into and developed knowledge and experience in. If credibility is about proving to others that you know what you are talking about, expertise in this context is about your own confidence that you know what you are talking about.

Your expertise will ideally have been validated by practical application in one form or another. While it's certainly possible to know a subject well without performing formal research in the area or earning professional achievements using your knowledge, practical experience will help you avoid a situation in which the questions you receive from your audience demonstrate that you don't know the topic as well as you thought you did.

Fortunately, as with credibility, your advanced degree gives you a head start in finding and validating your areas of expertise. Still, don't limit yourself to what you have studied in a formal academic capacity. We all have acquired knowledge and experience in areas that we have not specifically studied in a university setting, and this is a great opportunity to use it.

Going back to our earlier examples, I have experience in speaking about Martin Luther King Jr.'s legacy because I have done so before in both classroom and speaking engagement settings, so I feel confident in my ability to do so. The history of Black comic strips is an area of expertise for me because I did my dissertation on Black comic strips, so I know I have the knowledge and experience I need to speak on that topic with authority.

What You Want to Talk About

This quality is the easiest to understand—and also the easiest to overlook. What are you passionate about? What do you want to share with others? What do you think is important to spread the word about? Nothing is off-limits when thinking up your list of answers; they may not be what you studied formally, and that's okay. The last thing you want to do is book yourself a series of speaking engagements where you have locked yourself into speaking about something you have no interest in simply because it lines up with your degree. That's an example of you working for your brand rather than your brand working for you, and it's a surefire recipe for burnout. Both of my example topics above are subjects I love talking about and subjects I believe are valuable points of discussion.

Write down a list of at least five specific topics that match all three of these qualities. Try not to stress about your lack of demonstrable credibility in an area you have expertise in. The goal is not to create a long to-do list of awards you need to win or research you need to do in order to be ready for your speech. The goal is to create a list of narrow, actionable topics that you are already willing and able to speak about with authority. Keep it simple and cast a wide net, and you'll soon have a list you can start reaching out to your target audiences about.

Ingredient 2: The Target

In order to get a platform for your talk, you will need to pitch yourself, and for that you will first need to understand the two buckets your pitch's target audiences will fall into: hot/warm audiences and cold audiences.

Hot/Warm Audiences

Hot audiences are people you know and people who know you. These are people who you have personally spoken to before and that you have some sort of relationship with. Similarly, warm audiences are also people you know and people who know you. They are comparatively not as close to you and not regularly in touch with you, but they are still people you have a personal or professional connection to. Hot and warm audiences are very likely to open your email when they see it. This is why these people constitute your immediate network.

Gather at least thirty contacts from your immediate network that you will email and pitch your speaking engagement services to, focusing on those from the world of higher education and academia first. If you are wondering what kinds of people to include on this list, the contacts on my list include:

- Dr. Ron Jackson, with whom I wrote a book
- The twenty or so women I met during a week-long retreat I attended several years ago hosted by HERS, an organization dedicated to women's leadership in higher education
- People with whom I had lunch years ago and email once every six months

Dr. Jackson would definitely be considered a hot audience, while the others are warm audiences, but they are all a part of my immediate network because I believe they would all open an email from me as long as I do not take advantage of or abuse my relationship with them.

Cold Audiences

Cold audiences are people you have no personal or professional relationship with. You might be aware of each other's work, but you have never spoken to each other and are functionally strangers.

When it comes to cold audiences, there are four main buckets that our targets might fall into:

1. Student group leaders
2. Chairs of departments
3. Deans of schools
4. Any other heads of departments

These are the people who will be making decisions regarding who might be brought to campus for a speaking engagement. Don't overlook the student group leaders in this list. These are undergraduate and graduate students who run organizations on campus, and they may work closely with their student government association or heads of departments to bring in their speakers of choice, or—depending on their funding and leadership structure—they may even make decisions regarding guests unilaterally without needing faculty intervention.

These groups of people are who you need to get yourself in front of so that they know you are available for speaking engagements.

Make a list of at least fifteen contacts—names and email addresses—from these groups of people, making sure not to neglect universities that you have associations with.

Since you have a way in with the universities from which you earned your undergraduate or advanced degrees, I would encourage you to thoroughly research potential contacts from these schools. Focus on researching organizations and departments related to the list of topics you put together earlier. For example, if you want to speak about the impact of the coronavirus pandemic on the mental health of youth, find contacts related to campus mental health organizations and university psychology departments.

The other step we need to take to make the most of our cold audiences is to also write down three to five contacts for conferences or professional organizations where talks regarding the topics you have chosen would be appropriate. As we research and collect these contacts, we should be strategic about when we reach out to conference organizers for potential conference placement. Most conferences are held yearly and take a long time to plan and prepare for, so don't contact the organizers of a conference that's scheduled to occur in three weeks, because the speakers have likely already been determined. Instead, contact those same organizers six months before their annual conference.

Collating these lists of contacts may seem like a lot of work each time you are trying to book speaking engagements, but once opportunities start rolling in, less work will be required. As you get more and more speaking engagements, news coverage, and other social proof under your belt, you will find that eventually you won't have to reach out to conference organizers at all; instead, they'll be reaching out to you.

Ingredient 3: The Pitch

Once you know what to talk about and who to reach out to, all that's left is your sales pitch. For this, we will want to handle hot/warm audiences and cold audiences differently.

The Hot/Warm Audience Pitch

Our hot/warm audiences are people with whom we have personal or professional connections; thus we want to do our best so they don't feel like we are taking advantage of them or abusing our relationship with them.

Specifically, we want to make sure our emails to them don't feel fatiguing or purely transactional in nature. To that end, I recommend messaging them no more than once every six months, and even once a year would likely be enough.

Also, one bulk email to the whole list of hot/warm audiences is preferable to writing personalized emails to each person, as sending individual emails is not an efficient use of your time (unless you hire a virtual assistant to do it), and being transparent that you are messaging many people allows your emails to those you have not spoken with recently to feel less intrusive.

That being said, make sure that you use the BCC feature so that you are not sharing everyone's email address with every recipient on the list.

Finally, I recommend focusing the bulk of the email on letting your contacts know what you have been up to, your recent accomplishments, and your upcoming projects, and save your speaking engagement pitch for last. This simultaneously keeps the email from feeling too calculated, establishes social proof, and opens the door for collaboration with experts in your network.

Below is an example of an email that I sent to my hot/warm audience contacts in 2018—reproduced here verbatim—where you can see these tips in action.

Dear colleagues and friends,

I wish I could do a better job of keeping up with everyone. I have not talked with many of you in so long. I have been engaging in some interesting projects in 2018/2019, and I wanted to share them with you, as there may be room for collaboration, conversation, or mutual support. I am also available for speaking engagements in 2019.

It has been almost a year since the publication of my most recent book, *Encyclopedia of Black Comics* (Fulcrum Press, 2017), which was featured in the *LA Times* and *VIBE*. The *Encyclopedia* won numerous awards, including most recently, the 2018 PubWest best design award. In May 2018, I completed co-writing the critically acclaimed comic book *Superb*, about a Black female superhero and a teenage superhero with Down syndrome. The book was written with the support of the National Down Syndrome Society. It has been a wonderful transition to move from academic writing to op-ed writing for national publications on social justice and political issues, to writing-producing-directing a documentary film, to creative writing—writing a comic book.

I will continue to push myself to use creative writing and arts to advocate for marginalized communities.

I have a few exciting new projects coming up, one of which is a graphic novel about Black leaders in Philadelphia, which has been funded by the Pew Center for Arts & Heritage. The graphic novel will be written for the Philadelphia public schools system and introduce young people to icons such as Cecil B. Moore and W.E.B. Du Bois (*The Philadelphia Negro*). I look forward to writing *Black Lives Have Always Mattered: Hidden African American Philadelphia of the Twentieth Century*. The Charles Blockson collection at Temple University is heading up this project and selected me as the lead writer for the collection.

I have a few more projects in the works and I would love to find ways that you and I can connect on projects, talk more about common interests, and find ways to support one another.

Finally, I am booking speaking engagements for 2019 and would love to come to your university or be recommended through your network. I have included my short bio below and relevant areas/speaking topics:

- LGBTQ justice, politics, philosophy
- Race and higher education
- Sexual freedom vs. religious freedom
- Changing organizational culture to create more diverse spaces
- Creating safe spaces for LGBTQ youth

- Making yourself more valuable (a talk for high school students/early college focused)
- How to write comics, documentary filmmaking, script writing, and production
- Feminism, womanism, and Black feminism
- Politics and Black politics in the American political system
- Publishing edited/single-authored volumes

I am especially available for the following events:

- October: LGBTQ History Month/Diversity Awareness Month
- January: MLK Day
- February: Black History Month
- June 19: Freedom Day/Emancipation Day
- March: Women's History Month

If you are interested in having me serve as a guest speaker, panelist, or facilitator, or if you would like to talk about possible collaborations, please contact me.

You can find more information on my website at *www.sheena choward.com*.

Bio:

Sheena C. Howard, Associate Professor of Communication at Rider University. Howard is an award-winning author, filmmaker, and scholar, including a 2014 Eisner Award winner for her first book, *Black Comics: Politics of Race and Representation* (2013). She is also the author of *Black Queer*

Identity Matrix (2014), *Critical Articulations of Race, Gender and Sexual Orientation* (2014), and *Encyclopedia of Black Comics* (2017). Howard is co-writer of the critically acclaimed sci-fi comic book *Superb* (issues 1–9). Howard is the writer, producer, and director of the documentary film *Remixing Colorblind* (2016). *Remixing Colorblind* examines the ways in which the educational system shapes our perceptions of race. Howard has appeared on NPR (National Public Radio) and ABC-TV, *The Breakfast Club*, the *Washington Post*, *Philadelphia Weekly*, as well as other networks and documentaries as an expert on popular culture, race, politics, and sexual identity negotiation. Howard has op-eds in the *Huffington Post*, Philly.com, and more.

There are some things to note from this email.

- First, I am immediately clear with all recipients that I am emailing multiple people by opening with the salutation "Dear colleagues and friends."
- Second, I share all of my projects and accomplishments over the previous year as well as what I have planned for the next year.
- As I list accolades and coverage I have received, I make sure to link to them to take advantage of this crucial opportunity to establish social proof.
- Then, and only then, do I explicitly mention that I am available for speaking engagements in 2019, and I include a list of topics I am prepared to speak on. Some of these are narrow and specific, like the topics we decided earlier in this chapter, while others are broader. Once you generate your list of topics, you will be able to extrapolate certain broader areas that you feel

comfortable covering, so it is up to your discretion what kinds of topics you include in this list.

- Along with these topics, I provide a list of events and holidays from the US holiday calendar that my talks would be appropriate for. Academic institutions often bring in speakers for events and holidays—and even the ones that don't might consider doing so—and there are designated holidays for everything you can think of, from Mental Health Awareness Month to Mother's Day. The list you include will surely be different from the one I have provided here, but I do recommend including one, as it helps prime the reader to consider you when those conversations arise.

- Finally, I include a short bio of myself so that anyone reading has a quick and thorough context for my career if they need it.

Altogether, this is a winning formula for a pitch to book speaking engagements targeted toward people you have a relationship with already.

The Cold Audience Pitch

With cold audiences, we are beginning from a place of unfamiliarity, so personalization is encouraged. Anything you can do to establish a connection with the reader early on will go a long way toward making them amenable to your proposal. Below is an example email for cold audiences, reproduced in full, followed by some notes on how to use this as a template for your own email.

Dear John,

I've attended your conference in the past, and I have really enjoyed it. You are doing a wonderful job organizing.

Currently, I am seeking to fill out my campus tour for the fall 2016 and/or spring 2017 and I would like to discuss the possibility of bringing the film *Remixing Colorblind* to your university.

The film *Remixing Colorblind* serves as a conversation starter to engage with your campus community in discussing and implementing actionable items around diversifying the faculty body, creating campuses that are inviting for students of color, diversifying the administrative body, and thinking critically about how universities may reinforce harmful notions of race. Screenings also come with a small booklet, which addresses action items that campuses can take to address these issues, from cost-effective solutions to more "radical" ideas. With screenings, campuses can make copies of the book for the community administrators and faculty. The film also addresses implicit bias, reverse racism, and affirmative action, among other subtle issues.

My aim is to spark change on campuses across the country and internationally, in an effort to prevent college campuses from experiencing the types of fury that we saw at the University of Missouri. We know there are critical issues on college campuses that do not make it to public consciousness, but we can be proactive in changing campus climate. This is what I believe and this is why I created this documentary.

I hope that you will consider bringing the film to your university (for a screening and Q and A) or having your university library acquire the film. Attached is the media kit for the film as well as the price list options for bringing the film to your campus, plus my CV.

I would love the opportunity to come to your campus.

Let's break down the structure so that you can use this as a template for your own emails to cold audiences.

- I first open by finding a connection with the organization or event that I am contacting and paying them a compliment. This helps break the ice and shows that you are speaking directly to the recipient and care about your relationship with them.
- Next, I inform the recipient of the purpose of my email. LinkedIn reports that the average time spent reading an email is just ten seconds, so when messaging cold audiences, we want to make sure that the main purpose of the email is presented early in the message and easy to grasp.
- Then I explain what's in it for them. Remember, this is a sales email, so we don't want to rely on how great a booking would be for us in order to convince the reader. Instead, we want to show them how great it would be for them to book us. In this case, I am providing them with all of the resources and information they need to have a conversation that is otherwise difficult and daunting.
- After that, I explain how the topic I want to speak with them about is timely, relevant, and significant. If you can convince the reader that the information you want to share is relevant to the events of today, relevant to their own community's

experiences, and important information for them to have, then you are well on your way to closing the sale.

- Finally, I make my call to action. The same way that your purpose should be clear and comprehensible at the beginning of the email, the action you are asking the reader to take should be clear at the end of the email.

- I also include social proof in the form of my press kit and CV, which is essential. Using links and attachments, you can include interviews, press coverage, and high-quality recordings of prior speaking engagements.

In these pitch emails—for both hot and cold audiences alike—we can see our sales funnel in action. With all of the information you've just given them, they may well be poised to take you up on your offer. You want to make the path from awareness to action as effortless as possible.

Another Cold Audience Strategy

There is one additional strategy you can use to make contact with cold audiences. In the book *Originate, Motivate, Innovate: 7 Steps for Building a Billion Dollar Network*, which I co-wrote with the CEO of Black Girl Ventures, we talk about linkage, interest, and ability. The book states that:

- Linkage asks: *Are you connected to this person?*
- Interest asks: *Is this person interested in what you are working on?* and
- Ability asks: *Does this person have the ability to help or fund you?*

These questions are useful in framing the type of outreach you make and how you make it. It requires you to do research on someone who might be cold, such as the dean of a college who has the power to bring you in to speak. That dean doesn't know who you are, but if you research them, you can find an aspect that is a connection point (*linkage*).

This might mean that they are affiliated with an organization that you are affiliated with, or they know someone that you also know. You want to include this in your email outreach, as someone is more likely to take notice of your message if there is some commonality. *Interest* considers the notion that the person you are reaching out to needs to have an interest in your subject matter. This is important in terms of your rate of success. I wouldn't pitch my speaking engagement topics on, say, LGBTQ rights to the chair of a department at a conservative, Christian university. They may be interested in bringing me in, but that likelihood is a lot less than at a university that has a track record of bringing in speakers who talk about LGBTQ rights.

The goal is to increase your odds of getting hired. You don't want to try to sell something to someone who has no interest.

Finally, *ability* is considering if they are even a person to reach out to in terms of being capable of funding your speaking engagement. Knowing higher ed, you might know that this dean does have influence in this area. You are less likely to be successful if you are pitching yourself to individuals who have no influence in the funding side of it.

Implement this L.I.A. framework to increase your odds of success when making cold as well as warm/hot outreach.

In this chapter, we have explored what a sales funnel is and how you can implement the stages of a sales funnel to increase your speaking engagement opportunities. For whatever it is that you decide to monetize, you need to have a system in place to generate steady income. While building your brand will help you create a strong reputation, increase your visibility, and differentiate you from your peers, the key to increasing your income is a sales funnel system.

A sales funnel is a step-by-step process that takes potential clients from initial awareness of your brand to the point of making a purchase. It is important to note that a sales funnel is not a one-time event but rather a continuous process that requires constant optimization.

A well-designed sales funnel can help you build a loyal following, generate leads, and ultimately increase revenue. It enables you to nurture your leads and provide them with valuable information, which can help build trust and credibility. By consistently delivering high-quality content and engaging with your audience, you can convert leads into paying clients.

A sales funnel also helps you to understand your audience better. By tracking and analyzing their behavior, you can gain insights into their needs, preferences, and pain points. This information can be used to refine your branding strategy, create more targeted marketing campaigns, and ultimately increase your chances of success. As you look back on all that you have learned in this book, many of the activities, such as your social media strategy, have already prepared you to optimize your sales.

Building a strong reputation and standing out in today's competitive landscape is crucial for us academics as we navigate this fast-paced and ever-changing technological world. As such, by constantly optimizing your sales funnel and providing value to your audience, you can build a loyal following and achieve long-term success as an academic.

This book has taken you on a transformative journey through the three stages of the Power Your Research process: clarity, connection, and capital. I believe it is crucial to empower subject-matter experts to build their brands during this time of great change and uncertainty, when anyone can disseminate large amounts of information by using the accessible tools around us.

Part I emphasized the importance of following the Power Your Research process, cultivating a powerful mindset, and envisioning our goals outside of academia, all of which are crucial for navigating the ever-evolving landscape of brand building and academia. Chapter by chapter, we explored the significance of brand assets and how they contribute to our professional identity, recognizing that in an era of rapid transformation, subject-matter experts must proactively establish their unique voices and expertise.

In Part II, we delved into the world of connection, learning how to leverage social media strategies and media coverage to amplify our visibility. These tools and strategies are not only essential for building a strong personal brand but also for engaging with a wider audience, fostering meaningful collaborations, and disseminating knowledge to benefit society as a whole. In addition, we learned the power of a well-crafted brand that serves as an anchor in instilling trust and credibility between you and your audience.

Finally, Part III covered capital, revealing the value of building a dedicated following of true fans and understanding how to implement a sales funnel that generates income. By nurturing relationships with our audience, leveraging our expertise, and strategically positioning ourselves, we can move from where we are today to where we want to be in the most efficient way possible. Subject-matter experts that embrace increasing their visibility, authority, and income are not only positioning themselves to secure their own careers outside of academia but also to actively contribute to the advancement of knowledge and the transformation of society.

Armed with the insights gained from these pages, you are now equipped with the tools and mindset needed to forge your own path, enhance your own brand, and make an impact at scale. May this journey be the catalyst for a flourishing career both inside and outside of academia, filled with purpose, passion, and promise.

Acknowledgments

Will Toms, cofounder of REC Philly, thank you for being the first creative coach I ever had and leaving an impact on the way I think about building and monetizing my brand. Many of the concepts in this book were inspired by you. Thank you for sharing your journey with the world.

Mark Kanty and Jaimie Skultety, thank you for teaching me how to run a business and how to think like an entrepreneur. The program Upscale Your Business has changed my life forever.

Mike Ayalon, thank you for the value you bring to my life. Greek University has truly benefited the way I do business and the way I think about speaking engagements. You've helped me navigate the speaking circuit immensely.

Mahdi Woodard, the best online mentor I've never met, thank you. Over the last year, I've taken a number of your online courses on entrepreneurship and shown up to a number of your live videos. They have been incredibly valuable and transformational for me on my personal entrepreneurship journey. Even though I have never met you or worked with you in person, your content has provided tremendous value.

Thank you to the many coaches, mentors, and teachers who have believed in me along the way. There are too many to name, but know you have truly impacted my way of thinking.

Notes

1. American Association of University Professors. "The End of Faculty Tenure and the Transformation of Higher Education." AAUP, 2019, https://www.aaup.org/article/end-faculty-tenure-and-transformation -higher-education#.ZDlCo-zMLYI.

2. Cuff, Andrew. "Ph.D.s Need Real Data on How Potential Employers Make Hiring Decisions." *Inside Higher Ed*, May 3, 2017, https:// www.insidehighered.com/advice/2017/05/03/phds-need-real-data-how -potential-employers-make-hiring-decisions-essay.

3. Chowdhury, Arjun. "PhD Graduates Continue to Seek Tenure-Track Positions Despite Low Odds, Says Report." University Affairs, March 30, 2021, https://www.universityaffairs.ca/opinion/in-my-opinion/phd-graduates -continue-to-seek-tenure-track-positions-despite-low-odds-says-report/.

4. Best Colleges. "Statistics on Major College Closures." 2023, https:// www.bestcolleges.com/research/closed-colleges-list-statistics-major -closures/#:~:text=At%20least%2034%20public%20or,private%20 for%2Dprofit%20college%20closures. Accessed April 11, 2023.

5. Larson, R. C., N. Ghaffarzadegan, and Y. Xue. "Too Many PhD Graduates or Too Few Academic Job Openings: The Basic Reproductive Number R0 in Academia." *Syst Res Behav Sci* 31, no. 6 (Nov-Dec 2014):745-750. doi: 10.1002/sres.2210. PMID: 25642132; PMCID: PMC4309283.

6. Kabbaz, Michael. "Before Choosing a College, Make Sure It Will Exist in 10 Years." *Money.* December 18, 2020. https://money.com/colleges -closing-financial-stability. Accessed April 16, 2023.

7. Joynton, Natalie R. "Why Stop Seeking a Tenure-Track Job and Try Job Boards Instead." *Inside Higher Ed.* November 8, 2022. https://www .insidehighered.com/advice/2022/11/08/why-stop-seeking-tenure-track -job-and-try-job-boards-instead-opinion. Accessed April 16, 2023.

8. Vuong, Quan-Hoang, Thu-Huong Do, and Thu-Trang Vuong. "Resources, Experience, and Perseverance in Entrepreneurs' Perceived Likelihood of Success in an Emerging Economy." *Journal of Innovation and Entrepreneurship* 5, no. 1 (2016): 18.

9. Gottlieb, Carole S. "Fred Rogers (1928–2003)." *Encyclopedia of Children and Childhood in History and Society*, edited by Paula S. Fass, vol. 2, Macmillan Reference USA, 2004, 617–618. Gale eBooks, https:// link.gale.com/apps/doc/CX3429500583/GVRL?&sid=GVRL&x id=8aa8f7bb. Accessed March 19, 2023.

10. "Archetype Personality Types: Innocent Archetype." Know Your Archetypes. Last modified 2023. https://knowyourarchetypes.com/archetype -personality-types/innocent-archetype/. Accessed March 19, 2023.

11. Brown, Brené. "Brené Brown." https://brenebrown.com. Last modified 2023. Accessed March 19, 2023.

12. Duckworth, Angela. "Angela Duckworth - University of Pennsylvania." University of Pennsylvania. Last modified 2023. https://psychology.sas .upenn.edu/people/angela-duckworth. Accessed March 19, 2023.

13. Goodall, Jane. "Jane Goodall." Jane Goodall Institute. Last modified 2023. https://www.janegoodall.org. Accessed March 19, 2023.

14. Farmer, Paul. "Injustice Has a Cure," Partners In Health, https://www .pih.org. Last modified 2022. Accessed March 19, 2023.

15. Tyson, Neil deGrasse. "Neil deGrasse Tyson." Hayden Planetarium, https://www.amnh.org/explore/center-for-biodiversity-conservation /programs-initiatives/rare-disease-day/speakers/neil-degrasse-tyson. Accessed March 19, 2023.

16. Chomsky, Noam. "Noam Chomsky." Massachusetts Institute of Technology, https://linguistics.mit.edu/user/chomsky/. Accessed March 19, 2023.

17. Sagan, Carl. "Biographical Sketch." The Carl Sagan Portal, https://www.carlsagan.com/biography. Accessed March 19, 2023.

18. Ruffle, K. "7 Tips to Help Get Your Faculty Noticed by the Media." BlueSky Education, June 14, 2022. https://www.bluesky-pr.com/blog/business-education/7-tips-to-help-get-your-faculty-noticed-by-the-media?hs_amp=true. Accessed April 16, 2023.

19. Public Library of Science. "More Media Coverage of Scientific Research Linked to More Citations." Phys.org. July 1, 2020. https://phys.org/news/2020-07-media-coverage-scientific-linked-citations.html. Accessed April 16, 2023.

20. Godin, Seth. "Status Roles." *Seth's Blog.* February 21, 2018. https://seths.blog/2018/02/status-roles/#:~:text=Status%20roles%20are%20at%20the,less%20this%20or%20less%20that. Accessed April 16, 2023.

21. Edison Research. "The Infinite Dial 2021." Edison Research, March 11, 2021. https://www.edisonresearch.com/the-infinite-dial-2021-2. Accessed April 16, 2023.

Index

brand(s) (*continued*)
    color schemes and logos for, 11, 53, 130
    in Diffusion of Innovation theory, 102
    establishing your, 6 (*see also* brand assets)
    personal, 5
brand adjectives, 10–11, 82–84
    for consistent online presence, 83
    creating list of, 83–84
    purpose of, 54
brand ambassadors, 166–167
brand archetype(s), 10–11, 61–82
    Caregiver, 69–70
    Creator, 72–73
    determining your, 80–82
    explained, 62–63
    Explorer, 67–68
    Hero, 66–67
    Innocent Child, 64, 81
    Jester, 73–74
    Lover, 78–79
    Magician, 77–78
    Orphan (Everyman), 65–66
    purpose of, 54
    Rebel (Outlaw), 70–71
    Ruler, 76–77
    Sage, 74–76
    value of, 63–64
brand assets, 10–11, 53–86. *see also individual assets*
    alignment of, 150–151
    creating a brand statement, 54–61
    determining brand adjectives, 82–84
    example of, 60–61, 85
    identifying your brand archetype, 61–82
    in monetization, 150–151
    in social media, 90
    and "why" statement, 60
brand awareness, 164–168, 171–172
brand identity, 6, 53, 82

brand identity assets, 85. *see also* brand assets
brand persona, 53
brand personality, 63, 82, 91
brand statement, 10–11, 54–61
    defined, 55–56
    fit of brand archetype and, 81
    formula for creating, 56–59
    purpose of, 54
    using your, 59–60
The Breakfast Club, 48, 51, 121–122, 130
Brent, Derek, 91
brick-and-mortar stores, getting books into, 129, 130, 143–146
Brown, Brené, 15, 65–66, 119, 124
building equity, 12. *see also* monetization
building your platform, 140
Burton, Tim, 72

C
Caregiver archetype, 69–70
Charlamagne tha God, 121
Chomsky, Noam, 74–75
Chowdhury, Arjun, 13
Clance, Pauline Rose, 27
Coca-Cola, 165
cold audiences, 167
    identifying, 178–180
    linkage, interest, and ability strategy for, 188–189
    pitches to, 185–189
collaboration, 33
color schemes, 11, 53, 130
community
    insights into behaviors/preferences of, 91
    supportive of your mindset, 9–10, 29, 32–34, 150
    that needs your help, connecting with, 89
Crayola, 72
Creator archetype, 72–73

M
Magician archetype, 77–78
Mandela, Nelson, 69
Marquis Jet, 68
McDonald's, 165
media. *see also* social media
 high-level outlets, 46–47, 116–117
 refusing invitations from, 43
media blitz step, 12
media coverage, 111–128
 academic attitude toward, 22, 34,
  112–113
 high-level, 46–47, 116–117
 importance of, 112–114
 for increased visibility, 114–115
 with institution's media team, 26
 "Ladder Effect" for, 116–120
 pitching podcasts for, 122–128
 status roles for, 120–122
 vision keywords/phrases for,
  44–45
media placements. *see* outlets (media
 placements)
media strategy, 11–12
media team, institutional, 26
Merkel, Angela, 76–77
mindset, 9–10, 21–39
 finding community supportive of
  your, 9–10, 29, 32–34, 150
 and impostor syndrome, 27–32
 for monetization, 149–150
 and purpose statement, 34–39
 reframing your, 26
 scarcity, 32
 of self-promotion, 22–26
mission
 brand statement in, 54–55
 crafting your, 63
 in determining archetype, 80
Mister Rogers, 64, 81
monetization, 12
 by being of service, 23
 and brand assets, 150–151

and impostor syndrome, 30–32
and mindset, 149–150
offering audience value in, 151
1,000 True Fans model for,
  151–161 (*see also* 1,000 True
  Fans model)
as process, 149
sales funnel for, 163–191 (*see also*
  sales funnel)
and vision, 150
motivation, 33
MrBeast, 66

N
networking
 in awareness stage, 166
 in supportive community, 33
newspapers
 Ladder Effect with, 118
 local, 49–50
niche(es)
 benefits of, 168
 defining your, 166
niche outlets, 48–49
Nina's Whisper (Howard), 125–126
NPR, 49, 122

O
1,000 True Fans (Kelly), 151
1,000 True Fans model, 151–161
 concept for, 151–153
 with Fiverr.com, 154–158
 implementing, 153–154
 with social media, 158–159
 with Teachable.com, 160
online presence
 brand adjectives in, 83
 diversifying your, 166
 media placements in, 115 (*see also*
  visibility)
 with TEDx talks, 137–138
Originate, Motivate, Innovate
 (Howard), 188

INDEX

research citations, media coverage
and, 112, 113
resources, from community, 33
Rogers, Everett, 102
Rogers, Fred, 64, 81
Ruler archetype, 76–77

S
Sagan, Carl, 77–78
Sage archetype, 74–76, 81
sales funnel, 163–191
action items for creating, 171–174
action stage in, 170–171
awareness stage in, 165–168
desire stage in, 169–170
interest stage in, 168
and speaking engagements,
174–189 (*see also* speaking
engagements)
stages in, 164–165
scarcity mindset, 32
Scholar archetype, 74–75
search engine optimization (SEO),
123–124
self-promotion mindset, 22–26
example of, 25
meaning of, 19
reframing for, 26
self-published books, 144
SEO (search engine optimization),
123–124
Skultety, Jaimie, 36
social media, 89–109
brand adjectives for, 54
in brand-building process, 90–92
and Diffusion of Innovation
theory, 101–109
diversifying presence on, 166
media coverage vs., 111
for 1,000 True Fans, 158–159
3H strategy for, 11, 92–101
using your brand statement in, 59
social proof, 106–107, 168, 175
speaking engagements, 174–189. *see
also* TED Talks; TEDx talks

and impostor syndrome, 31, 32
pitches for, 180–189
posting videos of, 139
targets for, 177–180
topics for, 175–177
status roles, 120–122
Stein, Mark, 13
Stewart, Martha, 72
stocky website, 137
subject-matter experts, 17
submission guidelines, for books, 145
super fans, 152. *see also* 1,000 True
Fans model

T
target audience, 177–180
cold, 178–180, 185–189
in Diffusion of Innovation theory,
102–103
hot/warm, 166–167, 177–178,
180–185
for podcasts, 124
psychographics of, 57–58
Teachable.com, 160
TED Talks, 146
believing in yourself for, 134–136
proactive strategy for getting,
133–134
TEDx talks vs., 132–136
for visibility and impact, 136
TEDx talks, 119, 132–142, 146
believing in yourself for, 134–136
building your platform for landing,
140
local organizers of, 140–141
pitching, 141–142
proactive strategy for getting,
133–134
reason for choosing, 129–130
strategy for landing, 138–142
TED Talks vs., 132–136
for visibility and impact, 136–137
Temple, Shirley, 64
tenure, 13–16
thought leadership, 35

About the Author

Dr. Sheena Howard is a professor of communication, a writer, and creative entrepreneur. She is the first Black woman to win an Eisner Award for her first book, *Black Comics: Politics of Race and Representation*. She is the founder and CEO of Power Your Research, an academic branding company. She has written for DC Comics and Marvel. Her clients have included DMC (from Run-DMC), the founder of Black Girl Ventures Omi Bell, and many more celebrities, CEOs, and social-impact companies.